SpringerBriefs in

MW01716588

We are delighted to announce SpringerBriefs in Education, an innovative product type that combines elements of both journals and books. Briefs present concise summaries of cutting-edge research and practical applications in education. Featuring compact volumes of 50 to 125 pages, the SpringerBriefs in Education allow authors to present their ideas and readers to absorb them with a minimal time investment. Briefs are published as part of Springer's eBook Collection. In addition, Briefs are available for individual print and electronic purchase.

SpringerBriefs in Education cover a broad range of educational fields such as: Science Education, Higher Education, Educational Psychology, Assessment & Evaluation, Language Education, Mathematics Education, Educational Technology, Medical Education and Educational Policy.

SpringerBriefs typically offer an outlet for:

- An introduction to a (sub)field in education summarizing and giving an overview of theories, issues, core concepts and/or key literature in a particular field
- A timely report of state-of-the art analytical techniques and instruments in the field of educational research
- A presentation of core educational concepts
- An overview of a testing and evaluation method
- A snapshot of a hot or emerging topic or policy change
- An in-depth case study
- A literature review
- A report/review study of a survey
- An elaborated thesis

Both solicited and unsolicited manuscripts are considered for publication in the SpringerBriefs in Education series. Potential authors are warmly invited to complete and submit the Briefs Author Proposal form. All projects will be submitted to editorial review by editorial advisors.

SpringerBriefs are characterized by expedited production schedules with the aim for publication 8 to 12 weeks after acceptance and fast, global electronic dissemination through our online platform SpringerLink. The standard concise author contracts guarantee that:

- an individual ISBN is assigned to each manuscript
- each manuscript is copyrighted in the name of the author
- the author retains the right to post the pre-publication version on his/her website or that of his/her institution

More information about this series at http://www.springer.com/series/8914

Daniele Morselli

The Change Laboratory for Teacher Training in Entrepreneurship Education

A New Skills Agenda for Europe

Springer Open

Daniele Morselli
Faculty of Educational Sciences
University of Helsinki
Helsinki, Finland

This project has received funding from the European Union's Horizon 2020 research and innovation programme under the Marie Skłodowska-Curie Grant Agreement No. 654101.

ISSN 2211-1921 ISSN 2211-193X (electronic)
SpringerBriefs in Education
ISBN 978-3-030-02570-0 ISBN 978-3-030-02571-7 (eBook)
https://doi.org/10.1007/978-3-030-02571-7

Library of Congress Control Number: 2018958349

© The Editor(s) (if applicable) and The Author(s) 2019, corrected publication 2019. This book is an open access publication.
Open Access This book is licensed under the terms of the Creative Commons Attribution 4.0 International License (http://creativecommons.org/licenses/by/4.0/), which permits use, sharing, adaptation, distribution and reproduction in any medium or format, as long as you give appropriate credit to the original author(s) and the source, provide a link to the Creative Commons license and indicate if changes were made.
The images or other third party material in this book are included in the book's Creative Commons license, unless indicated otherwise in a credit line to the material. If material is not included in the book's Creative Commons license and your intended use is not permitted by statutory regulation or exceeds the permitted use, you will need to obtain permission directly from the copyright holder.
The use of general descriptive names, registered names, trademarks, service marks, etc. in this publication does not imply, even in the absence of a specific statement, that such names are exempt from the relevant protective laws and regulations and therefore free for general use.
The publisher, the authors and the editors are safe to assume that the advice and information in this book are believed to be true and accurate at the date of publication. Neither the publisher nor the authors or the editors give a warranty, express or implied, with respect to the material contained herein or for any errors or omissions that may have been made. The publisher remains neutral with regard to jurisdictional claims in published maps and institutional affiliations.

This Springer imprint is published by the registered company Springer Nature Switzerland AG
The registered company address is: Gewerbestrasse 11, 6330 Cham, Switzerland

Foreword

In the last three decades, entrepreneurship education has taken off as a subject of interest worldwide. It has developed from being a minor interest in business schools in universities to being an important consideration for educational policy makers at national and supra-national level. Entrepreneurship education has spread across the university and has become embedded in other subjects, such as engineering and the fine arts. It has grown across the educational system and today programmes can be found in elementary and high schools in many countries. Entrepreneurship education has also spread, from being an almost uniquely North American phenomenon, to being of critical interest to European nations and has become important within the educational policy agenda of many. For example, it has been growing rapidly as a subject of concern across the Chinese tertiary sector. Today in the United States universities are even building significant infrastructure to support activity at a level noticeable to the New York Times which claimed that, "*Where once the campus amenities arms race was waged over luxury dorms and recreation facilities, now colleges and universities are building deluxe structures for the generation of wonderful ideas. They and their partners in industry are pouring millions into new buildings for business, engineering and applied learning that closely resemble the high-tech workplace, itself inspired by the minimally partitioned spaces of the garage and the factory*" (*NYT 08/07/2016*). The skills agenda in entrepreneurship is a unique and significant phenomenon that has gained considerable momentum. The trend towards promoting entrepreneurial training and development within educational systems would appear to be driven by consequential changes to the nature of work and employment. Many countries now recognise the need to promote and support self-employment, small business management and technology innovation and have developed policy to encourage education in these careers.

Consequently, this book by Daniele Morselli is timely. The book begins by highlighting the development of the entrepreneurial skills agenda with a specific focus on the European context. In the first chapter, the author explains the skills agenda in Europe and highlights the European perspective on 'enterprise skills'. Identified within these skills are the current competences recognised by the

European Union as contributing to the development of an 'enterprising mindset'. He explains these competences and then progresses to discuss how this perspective of entrepreneurship education fits in to the prevailing research on entrepreneurship education. In the next chapter, he focuses more on how to assess enterprise and entrepreneurship competencies within educational contexts. He provides some examples on assessing initiative, particularly within the vocational training context, and considers the literature on the assessment of entrepreneurship education. From this base, he introduces the Change Laboratory, which looks in depth at Cultural Historical Activity Theory and how this approach facilities expansive learning. He argues that that learning theory needs to drive our underlying frameworks for research in entrepreneurship education and presents in an effective way this theoretical construct as a basis for a deeper understanding about learning through experience. He, in subsequent chapters, moves to introduce his research using the Change Laboratory as an approach to explore enterprise skills education in vocational training in schools with a particular focus on surveying. Remaining chapters in the book present the outcomes of his research exploring a change project through the eyes of teachers, students and other participants and explaining the validation of the work and reflecting on the process as a researcher. The final chapter in the book provides a deep appreciation of how enterprise skills can be developed through the Change Laboratory method and explains the challenges and opportunities encountered when implementing the method, as well as, explaining the training outcomes for students.

This book provides an excellent read for any educator in entrepreneurship education and it should be of particular interest to educators and researchers studying entrepreneurship education in schools. The concept of the Change Laboratory and the method of Cultural Historical Activity Theory should be of interest to researchers in entrepreneurship education more generally, even where the focus of their work is the tertiary sector. His work is insightful into many areas and provides a good basis to explore the European agenda in entrepreneurship education. It allows for a better understanding of the skills agenda and the competencies that have been developed by the European Union to guide educators in the development of programmes and associated funding requests. The particular research topic provides much depth focused on how to engage schools in real change projects while also allowing the researcher to conduct research. In my view, therefore, this book has much to offer the reader interested in the topic of entrepreneurship education.

Athens (OH)

Dr. Luke Pittaway
Copeland Professor of
Entrepreneurship, Ohio University
USASBE Entrepreneurship
Educator of 2018

The original version of the book frontmatter was revised: For detailed information please see correction. The correction to the book is available at
https://doi.org/10.1007/978-3-030-02571-7_8

Contents

1 The Research Hypothesis 1
1.1 A New Skills Agenda: A Policy View on Entrepreneurship 2
1.2 The Debated Concept of Entrepreneurship 6
1.3 Why the Theory of Expansive Learning for Entrepreneurial Education? 8
1.4 The Research Hypothesis 11
Bibliography 13

2 The Assessment of Entrepreneurial Education 17
2.1 The Assessment in Competence-Based Education 18
2.2 The Assessment of Key Competences 21
2.3 The Assessment of Entrepreneurial Education 24
2.4 Examples of Best Practices in Entrepreneurial Education 27
2.4.1 Module on Grant Writing 28
2.4.2 Introductory Course in Entrepreneurship 29
2.4.3 Course in Social Entrepreneurship 30
2.5 The Characteristics of Entrepreneurial Teachers, Assessing the Way They Educate for a Sense of Initiative and Entrepreneurship. The SIE Questionnaire 31
Bibliography 35

3 The Change Laboratory in Theory 37
3.1 Expansive Learning 38
3.2 Formative Interventions 43
3.3 Expansive Learning as Collective Transformative Agency 46
3.4 Expansive Learning as Concept Formation 49
3.5 Preparing a Change Laboratory 50
3.6 Designing Tasks to Promote Expansive Learning 53
Bibliography 56

4 The Change Laboratory in Practice 59
4.1 Historical Contextualisation 60
4.1.1 The Field Research 62
4.2 The Change Laboratory Workshops 63
4.2.1 First Workshop, 23 February 2016 64
4.2.2 Second Workshop, 2 March 2016 66
4.2.3 Third Workshop, 8 March 2016 69
4.2.4 Fourth Workshop, 15 March 2016 71
4.2.5 Fifth Workshop, 22 March 2016 72
4.2.6 Sixth Workshop, 5 April 2016 74
4.2.7 Seven Workshop, 5 April 2016 77
4.2.8 Department Council, 10 May 2016 79
4.3 The Follow-up Workshops 79
4.3.1 First Follow-up, 31 May 2016 79
4.3.2 Department Council, 14 October 2016 80
4.3.3 Second Follow-up, 22 March 2017 81
Bibliography 81

5 Participants' View on the Interdisciplinary Project 83
5.1 The Methodology 84
5.2 The Interdisciplinary Project in the Eyes of the Teachers 85
5.2.1 What Are the Historical Antecedents? 86
5.2.2 What Are the Features? 88
5.2.3 What Are the Potentials? 91
5.2.4 What Are the Challenges? 93
5.3 The Interdisciplinary Project in the Eyes of the Workshop Assistants 96
5.3.1 What Are the Features? 96
5.3.2 What Are the Potentials? 97
5.3.3 What Are the Challenges? 99
5.4 The Interdisciplinary Project with the Class a Students' Eyes 100
5.5 The Interdisciplinary Project with the Class B Students' Eyes 104
5.5.1 What Are the Features? 104
5.5.2 What Are the Potentials? 106
5.5.3 What Are the Challenges? 107
Bibliography 110

6 Reflecting on the Expansive Learning Process 111
6.1 The Interdisciplinary Project with the Member Checks 112
6.1.1 The Features of the Interdisciplinary Project 113
6.1.2 The Potentials of the Interdisciplinary Project 114
6.1.3 The Challenges of the Interdisciplinary Project 115

6.2 Is the Interdisciplinary Project Implemented According to a Competence-Based Approach? . . . 116
6.3 A Comparison Between the Interdisciplinary Project in the Two Classes . . . 119
6.4 The Interdisciplinary Project Facing a Tertiary Contradiction . . . 120
6.5 Old and New Curriculum . . . 121
6.5.1 The Old and New Coordination Among Teaching Staff . . . 122
6.5.2 Tensions Between the Old and the New Didactics . . . 123
Bibliography . . . 124

7 Conclusions: Towards Entrepreneurial Education Through the Change Laboratory . . . 125
7.1 The Story so Far . . . 126
7.2 Impact of the Change Laboratory Workshops . . . 130
7.3 A Double View of Entrepreneurial Education in the Process and in the Outcome . . . 132
7.4 Concluding Remarks. Towards Teacher Training in Entrepreneurship with the Change Laboratory . . . 135
Bibliography . . . 137

Correction to: The Change Laboratory for Teacher Training in Entrepreneurship Education . . . C1

Appendix A: The Interdisciplinary Project . . . 139

Appendix B: Results Validation . . . 143

Introduction

Audentes fortuna iuvat
Virgil

These words attributed to the ancient Roman poet Publius Vergilius Maro enjoy a widespread popularity and are often interpreted as instructing how fortune favours the bold. Modern education systems are confronting the issue of how to educate students to be creative, innovative, autonomous and able to take calculated risks when necessary. These are the attitudes concerning *a sense of initiative and entrepreneurship*, a European key competence for lifelong learning, which is defined as *the ability to turn ideas into action*. The literature argues that the teachers educate for a sense of initiative and entrepreneurship only when they are entrepreneurial themselves. How to the make the teaching staff entrepreneurial through in-service training is the question leading this book. The answer lies in the Change Laboratory, a type of formative intervention, where the participants discuss problems that are salient for them and their organisation. This process subsequently involves the participants collectively finding a new model or concept, progressively implementing it and then making these adjustments the new customary way to do things. This series of steps is the essence of expansive learning, a relatively new theory of learning, and this book shows how such theory can support entrepreneurial education.

At first sight, it may look contradictory that a Change Laboratory can lead to a precise objective, that is training teachers for a sense of initiative and entrepreneurship. As a matter of fact, formative interventions are opposed to linear intervention because the outcomes cannot be planned ahead, and the participants—not the researcher—are in charge of the intervention. However, the *Change Laboratory for in-service training is expected to create the conditions for teachers to act with a sense of initiative and entrepreneurship within their organisation.* Cultural Historical Activity Theory, the framework used in this research, argues for an enlargement of the unit of analysis from the individual to the organization and its network. Within this paradigm, the teaching staff engage in Change Laboratory workshops to question their present practices, analyse their activity, generate new ideas or concepts and collectively implement them, thus creating value for their school and community. It is maintained that the definition of entrepreneurship is expanded beyond business creation towards an entrepreneurial mindset that each of us should own to turn ideas into actions, a key competence for lifelong learning. Such a mindset is also necessary for teachers to deliver their subjects in an entrepreneurial way and acting as role model for their students.

The research questions explore the extent to which a Change Laboratory as in-service training can be useful for promoting a sense of initiative and entrepreneurship among the teaching staff. The argument is that the Change Laboratory has a double impact. The first type of impact is in the outcomes: the highly mediated environment of the Change Laboratory helps to generate a new concept or idea, which is then used to ensure purposeful implementation. The literature argues that teachers see entrepreneurship education as a method of pedagogical renewal and personal development; the Change Laboratory promotes pedagogical renewal and new teaching practices. The second type of impact this formative intervention has is in the process: by implementing the new solution the teaching staff develop their collective transformative agency and turn ideas into action. The conclusion is that *with the Change Laboratory for teachers in-service training, new ideas of pedagogical practices are transformed into collective action and value for the school and the students*. The students and the teaching staff learn *through* entrepreneurship rather than *about* entrepreneurship.

Besides the encouragement to be bold in life that was promoted in both ancient Italy and modern globalised societies, Virgil's maxim characterises this research since he was born in a little city in the Lombardy region, which is a similar context to where this empirical research was carried out. For a decade previous to this study, a course in surveying in a technical institute had seen a progressive drop in enrolments. In first semester 2016, a bold "gang" of teachers and workshop assistants engaged in a Change Laboratory to analyse the causes that led to such disastrous circumstances and find a shared solution. They cultivated an interdisciplinary project to be implemented during the 2016–2017 school year in two Grade 5 classes with active didactics. In school year 2017–2018, the interdisciplinary project was repeated and expanded, leading to more teaching hours within the subjects, a wider variety of subjects spanning from technical to humanities disciplines, better coordination between the teaching staff, and better didactics towards a fully competence-based approach. Additionally, the teaching staff started educating for the new type of surveyor as it has been called for by both the school reform and the changes in the job market which took place in Italy from 2007 to 2008. They did so by acting in an entrepreneurial way, with the impact on the students being that they developed initiative and entrepreneurship, so they can transition into a workforce calling for self-employed professionals to be able to self-organise and effectively work in teams.

The book is characterised by a double thread: the tensions between formative and linear interventions, and the tensions between policy documents on entrepreneurship, and how entrepreneurship is actually enacted and taught by educators. It has been written not only for a target audience of policy makers, scholars in entrepreneurship and in the Change Laboratory who want to know more about the methodology. It has also been written with the people responsible for the implementation in mind: for teachers, school directors and other educators who wonder how the teaching staff can teach for a sense of initiative and entrepreneurship in an entrepreneurial fashion. Effort has been to provide the theoretical underpinnings, so it reads as a manual for this form of pedagogy, in the clearest and most accessible way possible. Although a professional facilitator is needed to organise and conduct a Change Laboratory, with this book the intention is to help the schools who would like to implement the Change Laboratory to know more about this methodology and the results they can expect. Moreover, on Open Aire database the interested reader will find all the transcripts of the workshops.

The book is structured in seven chapters. Chapter 1 makes the case for this research. Within the new policy paper 'A New Skills Agenda for Europe', the European Commission has launched a revision of key competences, and special interest will be given to the promotion of entrepreneurial and innovation-oriented mindsets. The policy literature considers the positive side of entrepreneurship without questioning the concept and how it is enacted and taught by educators. Given the variety of interpretations of entrepreneurship, the chapter defines the closely related terms, especially entrepreneurial education, entrepreneurship education, enterprise education, a sense of initiative and entrepreneurship. The first chapter also explains why expansive learning, a relatively new theory of learning, is needed to back entrepreneurial education. This part of the book outlines the research hypothesis, the historical and cultural context of the research, as well as the problems that the group of teachers was confronted with.

Chapter 2 tackles assessment of entrepreneurial education. Given the paucity of assessment in the research literature, this component can be read as stand-alone chapter. Assessment plays a fundamental role in teaching, as it is the assessment and not the curriculum that characterises what and how students learn. The chapter draws on both literatures of competences and entrepreneurial education, and the key message is that assessment cannot be a "one size fits all" process, but should be tailored to the institution and environments, with the active collaboration of the stakeholders. The final part shows three examples of courses in entrepreneurial education with aligned learning outcomes, teaching and learning activities and assessment practices. This section of the chapter also reflects on how to evaluate the way teachers educate for a sense of initiative and entrepreneurship inside and outside the classroom. These conclusions are in part based on the SIE questionnaire that was experimented on the teaching staff who later joined the Change Laboratory workshops.

Chapter 3 gives an overview on the Change Laboratory, the model of workshop used in this study. Its theoretical underpinnings come from Cultural Historical Activity Theory, which enlarges the unit of analysis to activity systems and sees the possibility for expansive transformations. This is the theory of expansive learning, a theory specific for innovation and change of social practices. Formative interventions, especially the Change Laboratory, are workshop models designed to trigger cycles of expansive learning. These structures are based on two principles, double stimulation and ascending from the abstract to the concrete. During Change Laboratory workshops, interactions are often recorded, and expansive learning is later studied for the generation of concept formation and collective transformative agency. The chapter then focuses on what is needed to prepare and conduct the workshops, with an examination of the tasks to promote the specific expansive learning actions.

Chapter 4 describes the workshops to make the readers understand the impact of the research. The aim is to thoroughly and accurately describe the relevant contextual circumstances such as the context of the study, participants and connected experiences. A special focus is devoted to the tasks to trigger expansive learning actions. The chapter illustrates the field research and how the course in surveying was selected for the Change Laboratory. It then describes the seven Change Laboratory workshops where the participants modelled an idea of an interdisciplinary project. Finally, it documents the follow-up workshops that reflect on and evaluate the new idea, thus showing how the new practice can be consolidated.

As an activity system is object oriented, a better understanding of the interdisciplinary project must come as a result of drawing from the words of the people involved: teachers, students and workshop assistants. For each of these types of participant, Chap. 5 discusses the features of the interdisciplinary project, its potentials and its challenges. Furthermore, it takes advantage of the teachers' longstanding experience within their educational context to understand the degree of change that the Change Laboratory affected in relation to its historical background.

Chapter 6 continues the analytical focus that was introduced in chapter five. It concentrates on the interdisciplinary project, which is analysed with the words of the participants, whose views are discussed during a follow-up workshop. The participants also evaluate the extent to which the interdisciplinary project has been delivered according to a competence approach. The aim of these tasks is twofold: validating the research findings with a participant validation strategy and triggering the expansive learning action of reflecting on and evaluating the process, to comprehend what else needs to be learnt to address these areas. In the next school year, the interdisciplinary project will be better implemented by resolving tensions between the old and the new; this change, in turn, will help train the new figure of surveyor that the school reforms and the job market have called for.

Chapter 7 explains how the methodology of the Change Laboratory can educate teachers for a collective sense of initiative and entrepreneurship. The research recently published by the European Commission suggests that teachers will educate for entrepreneurship only when they will be entrepreneurial themselves. This chapter contends that a Change Laboratory educates teachers to be entrepreneurial in the outcomes and in the process. Moreover, by showing how an idea is being turned into action, the book has shown the participants' collective sense of initiative and entrepreneurship. The Change Laboratory has an impact on the teaching staff, the students and the organisation, the role of the management being key in sustaining the change effort. All in all, with the shift of the unit of analysis from the individual to a collective activity system, the Change Laboratory brings new insights into entrepreneurship education; entrepreneurship cannot merely be seen as an individualistic and economic phenomenon, but becomes a collective and social phenomenon where individuals face a problem that threatens their community. They take the lead and find a solution that creates value for themselves and their community. This view of entrepreneurship emphasises the dimension of the sense of initiative—while entrepreneurship is the key competence for participation, citizenship and personal fulfilment—for a new skills agenda in Europe.

Finally, I want to acknowledge the Horizon 2020 Marie Curie project is financed by the European Union (project number 654101). I also want to acknowledge the many people who helped me in this endeavour. I thank Yrjö Engeström, the principal investigator of this project, and Annalisa Sannino, his wife, for their precious advice. I praise the bold teaching staff who participated in the workshops and year after year strive to implement and better their interdisciplinary project. I am grateful with Jaakko Virkkunen and Anna Maria Ajello for their reflections and for having followed the organization of the workshops. I thank Massimiliano Costa and Umberto Margiotta for their fresh insights into the organisation of the book contents. Although I am the only author responsible for the contents, I feel grateful towards the 'thought partners' who, by reviewing the chapters, contributed to the dialogical engagement with my study and data, these are Professors Luke Pittaway (who also wrote the introduction) and Andy Penaluna, Liubov Vetoshkina, Hongda Lin, Terhi Esko, Juhana Rantavuori and Antti Rajala.

Chapter 1
The Research Hypothesis

Abstract This chapter demonstrates that for the effectiveness of entrepreneurship to be realised, the teachers must model initiative and be entrepreneurial themselves, so their students can acquire this skill. It starts by outlining A New Skills Agenda, with the European Commission launching a revision of the key competences with a special focus on to the promotion of entrepreneurial and innovation-oriented mindset. There is currently a need for a broader view of entrepreneurship beyond business creation. A sense of initiative and entrepreneurship represents a European key competence. It is part of a mindset for turning ideas into action which is transferrable to many contexts as well as being a lifelong learning perspective. Given the polysemy of entrepreneurship, the chapter defines the terms closely related to it: entrepreneurial education, entrepreneurship education, enterprise education, and a sense of initiative and entrepreneurship. Although entrepreneurship can be learned, research about how teachers should be trained and how they can teach in an entrepreneurial way is an underdeveloped area. Among the learning theories used in research to support entrepreneurial education, the theory of experiential learning has been the most extensively used. However, expansive learning is a learning theory of innovation and collective change of practices that is most suitable for entrepreneurial education. The Change Laboratory is a type of formative intervention useful to promote cycles of expansive learning, and it was challenged in the context of an Italian secondary school with a course in surveying that had been suffering a dramatic loss of enrolments after 2008. This study explores the extent with which a Change Laboratory as inservice training can be useful to promote a sense of initiative and entrepreneurship in the teaching staff.

Keywords Entrepreneurial education · Sense of initiative and entrepreneurship Research hypothesys · Change Laboratory · A New Skills Agenda

The first section shows the European policy agenda with a renewed interest in entrepreneurial education. Within the policy paper *A New Skills Agenda*, the European Commission launched a revision of key competences with a special focus on to the promotion of entrepreneurial and innovation-oriented mindset. While psychological research has failed to find specific personality traits characterising the

© The Author(s) 2019

D. Morselli, *The Change Laboratory for Teacher Training in Entrepreneurship Education*, SpringerBriefs in Education,
https://doi.org/10.1007/978-3-030-02571-7_1

individual entrepreneur, the literature suggests that entrepreneurship is a skill that can be learned. Research in entrepreneurial education has not yet shown which didactics are most effective with the associated learning outcomes. Beyond didactics, in entrepreneurial education it is important that teachers act as role models to educate their students to have a sense of initiative and entrepreneurship. However, teacher training in entrepreneurial education—as well as how to train teacher to teach entrepreneurship in an entrepreneurial way—is an underdeveloped topic in research.

The second section shows the debate around the terminology and the concept of entrepreneurship itself. A common agreement on the terminology is absent, and the risk of misunderstanding and confusion is substantial. This book will use: (1) entrepreneurial education as general unifying term; (2) entrepreneurship education as functional view of entrepreneurship, that is venture creation; (3) enterprise education as broad educational view, a mindset to help turn ideas into action in many contexts and in a lifelong learning perspective; (4) a sense of initiative and entrepreneurship is the outcome for entrepreneurial education.

The third section explains why a new theory of learning such as expansive learning is necessary to underpin entrepreneurship. While experiential learning has been extensively used in entrepreneurial education, there are issues with its application, for example learning is considered a process internal to the individual, and it is not clear how the four phases follow each other. By way of contrast, expansive learning is a theory of innovation and collective change of practices that is more suitable to support entrepreneurial education. It focuses on communities as learners, transformation and creation of culture, horizontal movement and hybridisation and the formation of theoretical concepts. The Change Laboratory is a type of formative intervention useful to promote cycles of expansive learning, thus change and innovation. Its results can be evaluated against the development and implementation of new ideas and concepts and the development of the agency of its participants.

The third section also describes the context of the research—an Italian technical school—and why a Change Laboratory was needed. The course in surveying had suffered from a dramatic fall of enrolments for 10 years, with the reduction of the classes from four to one. The teachers did not know what could be done to revitalise the course, but knew that a collective effort would be necessary. The research questions explore the extent to which a Change Laboratory intervention as in-service training can be useful to promote a sense of initiative and entrepreneurship in the teaching staff.

1.1 A New Skills Agenda: A Policy View on Entrepreneurship

Skills, a term used to indicate what an individual can do, understand and know, are a path to prosperity and employability (European Commission, 2016). In a global and fast-changing economy, it is the skills which determine the ability to drive innovation and competitiveness. Not only are the skills key for investments, but they also contribute to the virtuous cycle of growth and job creation. Yet there is the danger that vast parts of the European population are left behind and marginalised by the digital revolution and globalisation, thus threatening social cohesion. The European situation calls for help: 70 million EU citizens have limited writing and reading skills, and even more individuals lack basic numeracy and digital skills, putting these individuals at risk of joblessness, social exclusion and poverty. More than half of 12 million long-term unemployed individuals can be regarded as poorly skilled. Skills mismatches and ability gaps are also evident. While many individuals have jobs that do match their qualifications and skills, 40% of European employers find it difficult to find the skilled people they are looking for (European Commission, 2016). Less than a third of the European citizens have a university degree against 40% of the USA and 50% of Japan (European Commission, 2010). Too few individuals have the entrepreneurial skills and mindset necessary to start a business. Dealing with these skills challenges calls for important reforms and policy efforts in education and training.

A New Skills Agenda is one of the most significant work programmes at the European Commission. It focuses on three areas (European Commission, 2016): (1) improving the relevance and quality of skills training; (2) making qualifications and skills more comparable and visible; (3) advancing knowledge about skills and intelligence about what level constitutes competence, to enhance career choices. The acquisition of skills is a lifelong process which takes place in formal and informal environments starting when individuals are very young. Beyond the technical and specific skill set, employers are increasingly looking for transversal skills like the capacity to work in teams, solve problems and thinking creatively. The same skills, which are useful when considering starting a business, are often neglected in school curricula and are seldom evaluated formally in member states. To help more individuals to obtain better key competences, the European Commission in 2017 will launch a revision of the key competences framework.

The European Framework for key competencies represents the political agreement on what a learner should able to know and do at the end of compulsory education (van Woensel, 2008). Its main objectives are (European Commission, 2007): (a) identifying and defining a set of key competences useful for active citizenship, personal fulfilment, employability and social cohesion in a knowledge society; (b) supporting the member states and ensure that, by the end of compulsory education, learners have achieved a level of mastery over key competencies helping them in the progression for further learning and working life in a lifelong learning perspective; and (c) providing tools for policy makers, employers and education providers; and (d) to present a framework for further action at the European level.

Competence is defined as a combination of knowledge, skills and attitudes that are relevant to the context. The Reference Framework establishes eight key competences (European Commission, 2007): (1) communication in the mother tongue; (2) communication in foreign languages; (3) mathematical competence and basic competences in science and technology; (4) digital competence; (5) learning to learn; (6) social and civic competences; (7) sense of initiative and entrepreneurship; (8) cultural awareness and expression. These key competences are all relevant since each contributes to personal fulfilment in a knowledge society. Many of them interlock, overlap and support each other. Within the *A New Skills Agenda*, the European Commission (2016) has launched a revision of key competences with a special focus on to the promotion of entrepreneurial and innovation-oriented mindset, including the encouragement of concrete entrepreneurial experiences.

One of the most important changes in the transition from the twentieth to the twenty-first century has been the emergence of the knowledge economy (OECD, 2010) with a returned centrality of the small and medium enterprises (SMEs). New companies and SMEs are the most aggressive agents of innovation and change in the economy, since they introduce new products and services, more effective ways of working, but they also represent the major source of new jobs. Compared to large companies, SMEs have become key players for innovation since they can better recognise and exploit not only the opportunities coming from market, but also the technological and competitive changes. These changes can all be considered as part of the transformation that has occurred from managed to entrepreneurial societies. The managed society enjoyed mass production and stable employments in big companies, while the government—in partnership with employers and unions—would play a major role in regulating society and economy. Such contracts comprised a controlled labour market and a robust welfare state. The decreased influence of unions and large firms, the lowered ability of governments to raise taxes at times of fast-moving capitals, and an enhanced turbulence of the labour market culminated in the withdrawal of the welfare state.

The entrepreneurial society rewards a proactive search for opportunities, a propensity for creative adaptation, and a drive to turn ideas into action (Bahri & Haftendorn, 2006). In the near future, most job opportunities will come from the growth of new businesses, and young individuals will be asked to generate their employment opportunities. Inside companies, workers will have to be able to take responsibility and decisions, carry out tasks autonomously, act creatively and flexibly, and to constantly update their competencies. Beyond business, entrepreneurship will be pivotal for communities to solve the problems that the globalisation has brought.

Internationally, North America plays a leading role in entrepreneurship education and in high-growth enterprises (Volkmann et al., 2009), and entrepreneurship is considered the main creator of economic growth (Draycott & Rae, 2011). The huge economic contributions of companies such as Amazon, Google, Microsoft are unquestionable. Compared to other countries, America enjoys one of the most entrepreneurial friendly cultures and environments, as well as the longest tradition in entrepreneurship education, the main goal being implementing and commercialising research, innovation or knowledge linked to generation of income (Volkmann et al., 2009). The definition of entrepreneurship aligns with its role: "we define entrepreneurship education as developing the mindset, skill set, and practice necessary for starting new ventures" (Neck & Corbett, 2018, p. 10). In China entrepreneurship education is still in its infancy, but progresses are rapidly being made, with more and more courses at the university level.

In Europe, the emphasis of entrepreneurship education lies on fostering entrepreneurial capabilities and mindset, and on recognising the social importance of entrepreneurial activity. Entrepreneurship has been a top priority since the Lisbon agenda in 2000. New enterprises, especially SMEs, are thought to represent the backbone of Europe and the primary source of new jobs. To restore jobs and growth in Europe after the financial crisis, more entrepreneurs would be necessary. While in 2010 45% of European citizens were keen on becoming self-employed, this figure plummeted to 37% in 2012 against 56% of China and 51% of USA (European Commission, 2013). In Europe 2020 three out of seven flagships for a smart, inclusive and sustainable growth are specifically dedicated to entrepreneurship (OECD & European Commission, 2013). In compulsory education a sense of initiative and entrepreneurship should be taught across the curriculum both horizontally and vertically, to provide advancement throughout the education levels (European Commission, EACEA, & Eurydice, 2016).

While psychological research that sought to find common personality traits which characterise the individual entrepreneur has been heavily criticised (Autio, Kenney, Mustar, Siegel, & Wright, 2014; Kyrö, 2006), in the literature there is no doubt that entrepreneurship can be learnt (Valerio, Parton, & Robb, 2014). Research has, therefore, moved towards the pedagogy of entrepreneurship (Kyrö, 2006), with questions such as how humans learn to become entrepreneurial, how they learn creativity, learn to recognise opportunities and combine resources and opportunities in new ways, eventually create new ventures.

Research in entrepreneurial education has opposed traditional didactics (including regular lectures) against innovative methods (which are more based on action) often summarised as passive and active methods (Mwasalwiba, 2010). While traditional didactics considers the student a passive receiver and focuses on content and compartmentalised subjects, active didactics feature interdisciplinarity, collaboration and project work, and see the student as an active part of the learning process (Lackeus, 2015). For Komarkova, Gagliardi, Conrads, and Collado (2015) collaborative learning and learning by doing are the two most suitable didactics for entrepreneurship education with students' self-centred learning becoming more important. Teaching methods should also develop attitudes such as creativity, inclination to take calculated risks and manage uncertain situations with an increasing importance of learning from failure and making connections with the outside world. However, research in entrepreneurial education has not yet shown convincingly which didactics are most effective and the corresponding expected learning outcomes (Valerio et al., 2014).

Beyond active didactics, in entrepreneurial education it is of utmost importance that teachers act as role models to educate their students to have a sense of initiative and entrepreneurship (European Commission, 2014; Heinonen & Poikkijoki, 2006; Peltonen, 2015). For the QAA (2018), teachers inspire and motivate their learners to advance in enterprising and entrepreneurial behaviours, attributes and competencies. Similarly, Bahri and Haftendorn (2006) suggest that teachers should be trained to display same of the entrepreneurs' features by being enterprising in the way they solve problems or overcome resource constraints. Also Penaluna, Penaluna, Usei, and Griffiths (2015) comment that teaching staff should be innovative and entrepreneurial in their in the way they design and deliver courses, thus acting as role models for what this behaviour looks like. However, the role of entrepreneurial teachers and the way they should be trained has been the subject of only a small amount of research (Morselli, 2017; Peltonen, 2015; Ruskovaara & Pihkala, 2013).

1.2 The Debated Concept of Entrepreneurship

The policy literature considers the positive side of entrepreneurship without questioning the concept and how it is actually enacted and thought by educators. Jones and Spicer (2009) suggested a critical perspective to question the concept, which until recently has been mostly studied as market-based and individualistic phenomenon. As it is defined nowadays, almost anybody could be considered an entrepreneur. In doing so the entrepreneur becomes a 'sublime object', a rather attractive but ultimately empty figure. Moreover, it should be considered that up to 90% of the start-ups fail die within the first 5 years of life. Only recently scholars have started investigating the 'dark side' of entrepreneurship—failure—by studying the two sides of it: fiascos and frauds (Olaison & Meier Sørensen, 2014). For Tedmanson, Essers, Dey, and Verduyn (2015), entrepreneurship can be studied as two-sided edge phenomenon encompassing oppression and emancipation that stand in a dialectic relationship.

After having 'unmasked' the entrepreneur Jones and Spicer (2009) reconstruct his/her essence. Firstly, the role of the state must be considered, as it distinguishes what is enterprising from what is not (Anderson & Smith, 2007). This is because ethics play a key role in the phenomenon. Second, entrepreneurship is not based on sole individuals, and as such the myth of the lemonade kiosk is misleading. Entrepreneurship entails working with others, and the creation of the potential for others to innovate rather than claiming innovation for themselves. Jones and Spicer (2009) conclude that characterising feature of entrepreneurship is about creating the enterprising potential for the others.

A group of scholars in the Nordic countries proposed the concept of pedagogical entrepreneurship to overcome the resistance of teachers towards the economic and business sides of entrepreneurship (Dal, Elo, Leffler, Svedberg, & Westerberg, 2016; Haara & Jenssen, 2016; Peltonen, 2015; Riese, 2010; Svedberg, 2010). The tensions between a narrow concept and a broad concept of entrepreneurship, which in the Nordic countries is seen as internal versus external entrepreneurship, have resulted in the growth of a wide array of approaches (Haara & Jenssen, 2016). The literature review on pedagogical entrepreneurship suggests bewilderment among educators, who find it difficult to define the concept in light of their educational practices (Dal et al., 2016). Many teachers perceive it just as another buzzword rather than an effective learning approach. In the literature, there is conflict and uncertainty about the framing of the concept, which presents fragmented and with no common starting point, except common referral to supranational policies. There are four challenges that characterise research on pedagogical entrepreneurship (Haara, Jenssen, Fossøy, & Ødegård, 2016). Firstly, coherence is missing between the aims of policy makers and actual implementation in schools. Second, the teachers stress the need for coordination among teaching staff to implement entrepreneurship, especially as it is a concept that challenges several older educational doctrines. The third challenge is teachers' insufficient knowledge about entrepreneurship. Fourth, the tensions between the programme that students are offered within the school and the increased attention on the activities 'out in the world' (Seikkula-Leino, Satuvuori, Ruskovaara, Hannula, & McCracken, 2015). For Haara and Jenssen (2016), pedagogical entrepreneurship should move beyond business creation towards human development with an emphasis on authentic activities, action and self-regulation. In other words, students should not learn *about* entrepreneurship but *through* entrepreneurship.

As stated above, finding a common agreement on the terminology is difficult, and therefore, the risk of misunderstanding and confusion is substantial. In research, entrepreneurial, entrepreneurship and enterprise education are often used without a clear rationale (Draycott & Rae, 2011; Mwasalwiba, 2010). Any discussion should, therefore, begin with a clarification of the terms used (Lackeus, 2015). In research, entrepreneurship education is often used as generic term to embed the other similar processes seeking to influence people's intentions, values, attitudes and behaviours towards entrepreneurship (Mwasalwiba, 2010). To avoid misunderstandings, this book will use entrepreneurial education as the unifying term embedding the other similar processes as suggested by Erkkilä (2000) and later by Lackeus (2015), and distinguish between entrepreneurship and enterprise education as from the UK Quality Assurance Agency. Enterprise education is defined as "the process of developing students in a manner that provides them with an enhanced capacity to generate ideas, and the behaviours, attributes, and competencies to make them happen" (QAA, 2018, p. 9). Instead, entrepreneurship education builds "upon the enterprising competencies of students who are capable of identifying opportunities and developing ventures, through becoming self-employed, setting up new businesses or developing and growing part of an existing venture" (p. 9). Table 1.1 draws from Jones and Iredale (2010) and displays the main differences between entrepreneurship education and enterprise education.

For Draycott and Rae (2011), enterprise education can be considered as a way to bridge the long-standing gap between the world of work of the real economy and education. It advocates liberal ideals with personal freedom and citizenship at the centre, since the individual has freedom to change, develop, grow and adapt to contexts, circumstances and contexts (Jones & Iredale, 2010). It promotes freedom, as it argues for the right to start own business, and citizenship, with an active pedagogical approach and a democratic learning environment. Draycott, Rae, and Vause (2011) suggest that an enterprising pedagogy should be flexible, traceable and with the students progressively taking control over their learning. One of the objectives of enterprise education is to contribute breaking the culture and the cycle of poverty to trigger communitarian and socio-economic regeneration (Jones & Iredale, 2014). However, entrepreneurship and enterprise education share value creation as a common goal; this can be either social, cultural or financial (Lackeus, 2015). The creation of value happens extensively in society and is closely linked with an individuals' happiness: any individual may help others make a living, but their self-worth also results

Table 1.1 Comparison between UK entrepreneurship education and enterprise education

Focus of entrepreneurship	Focus of enterprise
How to start a business including the key processes of business start-up	An active learning enterprise education pedagogy
How to plan and launch a new business venture	Knowledge needed to operate effectively as a consumer, citizen, employee or self-employed individual in a fast-changing market economy
How to grow and manage a business	The development of personal attributes, behaviours and skills to be used in numerous contexts
Enhancing the necessary skills and behaviours needed to run a business	The person as an enterprising individual—in the workplace, in the community, at home, or as an entrepreneur
The deployment of entrepreneurial skills and knowledge in a business context	The use of enterprising attributes, skills and behaviours throughout the whole life course
Imminent use of the knowledge and skills needed to start a business; and self-employment	How a business, particularly a small business works

Source Jones and Iredale (2010, pp. 10–11)

from a feeling of satisfaction due to participation, engagement and meaningfulness in relation to their life as a whole.

In contrast to America where entrepreneurship concentrates on new venture creation (Neck & Corbett, 2018), in Europe a sense of initiative and entrepreneurship is a key competence for lifelong learning. Very similarly with the QAA's definition of enterprise education, it concerns the capacity to turn ideas into actions (European Commission, 2007).

Coherently with the definitions above, this book will use: (1) entrepreneurial education as general unifying term, (2) entrepreneurship education as a functional view of entrepreneurship, that is with an eye to venture creation, (3) enterprise education as broad educational view, a mindset for proactive and self-reliant citizens who are capable of turning ideas into action in many contexts and in a lifelong learning perspective; (4) a sense of initiative and entrepreneurship is the outcome for entrepreneurial education.

1.3 Why the Theory of Expansive Learning for Entrepreneurial Education?

In entrepreneurial education, many researchers have speculated about the learning processes that support entrepreneurship. For Man (2006), the ability to learn is key to developing an entrepreneurship competence. Minniti and Bygrave (2001) observed that learning is a key feature of entrepreneurship: "a theory of entrepreneurship requires a theory of learning" (p. 1). Of the 16 contemporary theories of adult learning identified by Illeris (2009), only few have been used in the literature to support entrepreneurship education. According to Wang and Chugh (2014), the most used learning theories in entrepreneurial education are Lave and Wenger's (1991) situated learning, Wenger's (1998) community of practices, Kolb's (1984) experiential learning and Mezirow's (1997) transformative learning. For example, Mezirow's (1997) theory is used by Cope (2005) to emphasise how major challenges are imbued with emotions. Cope (2005) also applied the theory of situated learning (Lave & Wenger, 1991) to describe the contextual dimension of entrepreneurial learning and to study entrepreneurs as practitioners operating within multiple communities of practice.

Since entrepreneurship is intrinsically an experiential phenomenon, it is not surprising that Kolb's theory of experiential learning has been the most used to describe the entrepreneurial learning process. Of 75 articles reviewed by Wang and Chug (2014), 32 refer to experiential learning in a broader sense. Of these 32 articles, 14 refer specifically to the theory of Kolb (1984). When used broadly, experiential learning deals with learning by doing and by participating, learning from the others' experience, learning from favourable or adverse experiences and learning from the past (Wang & Chug, 2014). When used as indicated by Kolb (1984), experiential learning is considered a cyclic process composed of four dialectically related stages of reflection and action: concrete experience; reflective observation; abstract conceptualisation; and active experimentation (Wang & Chug, 2014). However, there are issues with Kolb's theory (Morselli, Costa, & Margiotta, 2014), as it was originally developed to be a classification to support the Learning Style Inventory (Engeström & Sannino, 2012), and its theoretical foundations are not solid (Miettinen, 2000). Firstly, it is unclear why the four phases follow one another in the recommended sequence (Engestrom & Sannino, 2012). Secondly, Kolb considers learning as an internal process. As a result of this assumption, his theory of experiential learning does not consider the social dimension of the learning process. For Gosen and Washbush (2004), during the last twenty years experiential learning has been used as a kind of "postmodern fantasy", that is "a Rousseauist invitation for students to return to nature and their genuine cleverness" (in Vozikis, Solomon, Winkel, Rideout, & Gray, 2013, p. 371). Similarly, Wenger's (1998) theory of the community of practices does not back adequately entrepreneurial learning, since it conceives learning as "one-way movement from incompetence to competence, with little serious analysis devoted to horizontal movement and hybridisation" (Engeström & Sannino, 2010, p. 2).

Many authors are, however, dissatisfied with the present learning theories because they do not offer an appropriate framework to underpin entrepreneurial education (Deakins & Wyper, 2010). By contrast, a suitable theory can be expansive learning, another of the 16 contemporary theories of adult learning identified by Illeris (2009). Within Cultural Historical Activity Theory (CHAT), expansive learning focuses on "communities as learners, on transformation and creation of culture, on horizontal movement and hybridisation, and on the formation of theoretical concepts" (Engestrom & Sannino, 2010, p. 2). Expansive learning is a theory of innovation and collective change of practices where "learners learn something that is not yet there"

(p. 2). During expansive transformations the contradictions of an activity system become aggravated, and some members start questioning and diverging from the established norms. As more practitioners join in, they engage in a collective design effort to conceive a new model of their organisation, and they move to implement the new model while improving and adjusting it. Ideally, a cycle of expansive learning is composed by learning actions which follow one other logically (Engeström, 2015): to question current practices, to analyse the situation with 'why' questions and explanations, to model the new explanatory relationship, to examine the new model and experiment it, to implement the model in practice, to reflect on the model and evaluate the expansive learning process, to consolidate the model into a stabilised practice and generalise it.

Based on this cycle, Engestrom (1994) describes learning as having three features. Firstly, learning is a meaningful construction and a creative use of cognitive tools; the tools can be external instruments or internal mental models. Secondly, learning is dialogue, participation and collaboration in communities of practice. Thirdly, learning can take the shape of criticism of the already existing practices, and this can spur innovation with creation of new ideas, artefacts and behaviours. Put in this way, there is a connection between the theory of expansive learning and the theories which study entrepreneurship as a broad phenomenon well beyond business creation. An example is Kyrö's (2006) cultural approach, which connects entrepreneurship to democracy, liberalism and economic development. Entrepreneurship is valuable during transitions in human history, where ideas of freedom and the need for new practices become vital for the society. In these periods, the role of entrepreneurship is to help dismantle and adapt the old institutions and systems so they become more flexible, and to create new practices.

Moreover, some authors utilised expansive learning to explain entrepreneurship as a process. Kauppinen and Juho (2012), for example, utilised expansive learning as a conceptual framework to show how entrepreneurial interactions between SMEs build international business opportunities. Mainela, Puhakka, and Servais (2015) conceptualised international opportunities in entrepreneurship as boundary crossing that is expansive transformations between related activity systems. In a Change Laboratory intervention, Barma, Laferrière, Lemieux, Massé-Morneau and Vincent (2017) documented the expansive learning actions that led a collectiveness to a successful entrepreneurial experience. However, expansive learning can be used beyond explanative purposes, since it is useful to bring about change and innovation, and in doing so it becomes a suitable learning theory to support entrepreneurial education (Morselli et al., 2014). As Chap. 3 will explain, within CHAT framework formative interventions have been designed to trigger cycles of expansive learning (Sannino, 2011). There are significant differences between traditional training courses called 'linear interventions' and 'formative interventions' developed within the Vygotskian legacy (Engestrom, 2011; Yrjö Engestrom, Sannino, & Virkkunen, 2014). In linear interventions, the structure and objective of the course are known ahead. By contrast, in formative interventions the participants deal with a contradictory problem with no apparent solution. In linear interventions, the researcher aims to gain control over the variables and the situation, whereas in formative interventions he or she aims to provoke and sustain an expansive learning process of transformation which is guided and owned by the learners.

The Change Laboratory is a type of formative intervention developed from the 1990s at the Helsinki University to promote deep and intensive transformations as well as incremental improvement (Engestrom, Virkkunen, Helle, Pihlaja, & Poikela, 1996). During Change Laboratory workshops a group of practitioners met for a couple of hours on a weekly basis for roughly 10 weeks as well as attending follow-up workshops for an intensive analysis of their activity system in a highly mediated environment. The instruments of the Change Laboratory were devised to analyse the relationships within and between activities, promote theoretical thinking and design new systemic structures (Virkkunen & Ahonen, 2011). The main tool is a 3 × 3 set of writing surfaces to display work activities used according to a horizontal and a vertical dimension, as Chap. 3 will explain. The results of this Change Laboratory can be evaluated in the light of: a) the process of development and implementation of new ideas and concepts; b) the development of the participants' agency from individual to collective actions, and from resistance and criticising to commitment and actions to change the organisation (Sannino, Engestrom, & Lemos, 2016).

1.4 The Research Hypothesis

There are, however, important preconditions for setting a Change Laboratory, the main one being, an activity system has to face a major change (Sannino, Engestrom, & Lahikainen, 2016). This means that a formative intervention would make no sense if the practitioners—teachers in this case—would not face a problem of value for them that could only be tacked with a collective effort. The research described in this study was carried out in a secondary vocational institute located in the Lombardy region in Italy. The school has three courses: graphics and communication, surveying, and logistics, for an overall number of 1000 students. The school was founded in the early 70s, and at that point in time it was exclusively structured to train future building surveyors. With the educational reform of 2008, the school introduced the other two courses, but while logistics has not yet taken over—it has been difficult some years to make one Grade 1 class, the course in graphics and communication had been growing year after year, moving from one to four Grade 1 classes. Unfortunately, such success had been counterbalanced by the drop of enrolments in surveying, who had moved from four Grade 1 classes in 2007 to one Grade 1 class in 2016.

As it will be described in Chap. 4, there have been historical reasons that caused the drop of new enrolments in surveying. Some of these were external to the school's dynamics, for example the crisis of the estate sector that led the profession of surveyor being a less attractive profession in the mind of the public, and the partial tertiarisation of the surveying profession.

This situation had created on the one hand a condition of helplessness of the surveying teachers, who did not know how to contain the loss of enrolments. On the other hand, the situation created a culture of blame, where external circumstances were labelled as the root cause for enrolment issues which cultivated an atmosphere of helplessness. Additionally, the school director was blaming the teachers for not having updated their study programme and didactics because of the school reform of 2008, with tedious lectures and unnecessary structural calculations making the surveying course overly ambitious and too difficult. In turn, the teachers blamed the school director for not having helped to contain the loss of Grade 1 surveying students; it was as if with her choices she had privileged the other school courses over the years. The teachers resisted her proposals and limited their participation in school extra-curricular activities and governance. Surveying teachers also blamed each other for not cooperating and admitted that such lack of collegiality impoverished the quality of their course. They also blamed the turnover of workshop assistants, the lack of workshops and of up-to-date equipment. Moreover, they blamed their colleagues in graphics and communication for taking all the enrolments with an unfair competition. Many surveying teachers considered the course in graphics and communication as a simplified version of surveying. As with surveying it was about drawing, yet it also dealt with activities such Internet, Facebook and Photoshop that appealed to the students. Unlike surveying it did not have complicated structural calculations.

This condition of blaming and helplessness created the conditions and need to set up a Change Laboratory. The teachers in surveying did not know what could be done to revitalise the course, but knew that a collective effort would have been necessary to change deeply the surveying course. At the same time, they knew that an answer for their problem could not come from the school director and they had to take the lead of the situation. When the researcher proposed the surveying teaching staff (both teachers and workshop assistants) to engage in Change Laboratory workshops they were happy to enrol. The goal was to find and implement shared solutions to revitalise the enrolments in surveying. Concerning the school director, she saw a Change Laboratory intervention as an opportunity both to promote the school outside (thus improving enrolments) and encourage concrete change within the school. She suggested that the best use of it would have been with the surveying course. Moreover, in order to let the teaching staff discuss freely and avoid resistance to her proposals, she participated in the workshops only at a later stage. In other words, she only joined in when the teachers had moved from the expansive learning actions of criticising and analysing the situation to modelling a new solution and committing for change.

A first expected impact of the Change Laboratory is to increase the number of Grade 1 students' enrolments in surveying. Beyond that, this research *explores the extent to which a Change Laboratory intervention as in-service training can be useful for promoting a sense of initiative and entrepreneurship among the teaching staff*. The research question is:

> To what extent can a Change Laboratory help the teaching staff turn ideas into actions? (RQ1).

The expression "to turn ideas into action" represents the definition of a sense of initiative and entrepreneurship as from the European Commission (2007). It is maintained that by showing a sense of initiative and entrepreneurship in the school, the teaching staff will act as role model for their students and thus teaching entrepreneurship by showing a sense of initiative and entrepreneurship as recently suggested by the literature (European Commission, 2014; Heinonen & Poikkijoki, 2006; Penaluna et al., 2015; Ruskovaara & Pihkala, 2015).

In conclusion, while many authors think that entrepreneurship is about business creation, this chapter has shown an enlarged definition that encompasses a sense of initiative and entrepreneurship, where everybody should be entrepreneurial at any stage of life and in any context. Additionally, teachers in schools could be entrepreneurial for themselves and for their students. The historical conditions and accumulated tensions that had led the course in surveying almost disappear had created a favourable setting to carry out a Change Laboratory, with the teachers deeply involved and ready to engage in a collective change effort to change their circumstances. Moreover, the workshops will permit the teacher to find their own meaning of entrepreneurship. In other words, rather than learning entrepreneurship with an "about" approach, the teachers will learn with a "through" approach to entrepreneurship. The next chapter returns to entrepreneurial education and its assessment. It will also explain useful concepts, including *about* and *through* approaches to entrepreneurship. The chapter shows three best practice examples of linear interventions for the delivery of entrepreneurial education, including the SIE questionnaire, which assists in evaluating the way teachers educate for a sense of initiative and entrepreneurship and can pave the way for a formative intervention.

Bibliography

Anderson, A. R., & Smith, R. (2007). The moral space in entrepreneurship: An exploration of ethical imperatives and the moral legitimacy of being enterprising. *Entrepreneurship and Regional Development, 19*(6), 479–497.

Autio, E., Kenney, M., Mustar, P., Siegel, D., & Wright, M. (2014). Entrepreneurial innovation: The importance of context. *Research Policy, 43*(7), 1097–1108.

Bahri, S., & Haftendorn, K. (2006). *Towards an entrepreneurial culture for the twenty-first century: Stimulating entrepreneurial spirit through entrepreneurship education in secondary school*. Paris: UNESCO Publishing.

Barma, S., Laferrière, T., Lemieux, B., Massé-Morneau, J., & Vincent, M.-C. (2017). Early stages in building hybrid activity between school and work: The case of PénArt. *Journal of Education and Work, 30*(6), 669–687.

Cope, J. (2005). Toward a Dynamic Learning Perspective of Entrepreneurship. *Entrepreneurship: Theory & Practice, 29*(4), 373–397.

Dal, M., Elo, J., Leffler, E., Svedberg, G., & Westerberg, M. (2016). Research on pedagogical entrepreneurship—A literature review based on studies from Finland, Iceland and Sweden. *Education Inquiry, 7*(2), 30036.

Deakins, D., & Wyper, J. (2010). A longitudinal and dynamic approach to entrepreneurial learning. *New Zealand Journal of Employment Relations, 35*(1), 35–47.

Draycott, M. C., & Rae, D. (2011). Enterprise education in schools and the role of competency frameworks. *International Journal of Entrepreneurial Behavior & Research, 17*(2), 127–145.

Draycott, M. C., Rae, D., & Vause, K. (2011). The assessment of enterprise education in the secondary education sector: A new approach? *Education & Training, 53*(8–9), 673–691.

Engestrom, Y. (1994). *Training for change: New approach to instruction and learning in working life*. International Labour Office Geneva.

Engestrom, Y. (2011). From design experiments to formative interventions. *Theory & Psychology, 21*(5), 598–628.
Engeström, Y. (2015). Learning by expanding: Cambridge University Press.
Engestrom, Y., & Sannino, A. (2010). Studies of expansive learning: Foundations, findings and future challenges. *Educational Research Review, 5*(1), 1–24.
Engestrom, Y., & Sannino, A. (2012). Whatever happened to process theory of learning? *Learning, Culture, and Social Interaction, 1*, 45–56.
Engestrom, Y., Sannino, A., & Virkkunen, J. (2014). On the methodological demands of formative interventions. *Mind, Culture & Activity, 21*(2), 118.
Engestrom, Y., Virkkunen, J., Helle, M., Pihlaja, J., & Poikela, R. (1996). The change laboratory as a tool for transforming work. *Lifelong Learning in Europe, 1*(2), 10–17.
Erkkilä, K. (2000). *Entrepreneurial education: Mapping the debates in the United States, the United Kingdom and Finland*. Abingdon: Taylor & Francis.
European Commission. (2007). *European competences for lifelong learning*. Luxembourg: Publication Office of the European Union.
European Commission. (2010). *Communication from the commission. Europe 2020. A strategy for smart, sustainable and inclusive growth.* Brussels Retrieved from http://ec.europa.eu/europe2020/europe-2020-in-a-nutshell/index_it.htm.
European Commission. (2013). *Entrepreneurship 2020 action plan. Reigniting the entrepreneurial spirit in Europe.* Retrieved from http://eur-lex.europa.eu/legal-content/EN/TXT/PDF/?uri=CELEX:52012DC0795&from=EN.
European Commission. (2014). *Entrepreneurship education. A guide for teachers.* Bruxelles: Unit entrepreneurship 2020.
European Commission. (2016). *A new skills agenda for Europe.* Retrieved from http://ec.europa.eu/social/main.jsp?catId=1223.
European Commission, EACEA, & Eurydice. (2016). *Entrepreneurship education at school in Europe. Eurydice report*. Luxembourg: Publication Office of the European Union.
Gosen, J., & Washbush, J. (2004). A review of scholarship on assessing experiential learning effectiveness. *Simulation & Gaming, 35*(2), 270–293.
Haara, F. O., & Jenssen, E. S. (2016). Pedagogical entrepreneurship in teacher education—What and why? *Tímarit um uppeldi og menntun, 25*(2), 183–196.
Haara, F. O., Jenssen, E. S., Fossøy, I., & Ødegård, I. K. R. (2016). The ambiguity of pedagogical entrepreneurship—The state of the art and its challenges. *Education Inquiry, 7*(2), 29912.
Heinonen, J., & Poikkijoki, S.-A. (2006). An entrepreneurial-directed approach to entrepreneurship education: Mission impossible? *Journal of Management Development, 25*(1), 80–94.
Illeris, K. (2009). *Contemporary theories of learning: Learning theorists... in their own words.* New York: Routledge.
Jones, B., & Iredale, N. (2010). Enterprise education as pedagogy. *Education & Training, 52*(1), 7–19.
Jones, B., & Iredale, N. (2014). Enterprise and entrepreneurship education: Towards a comparative analysis. *Journal of Enterprising Communities: People and Places in the Global Economy, 8*(1), 34–50.
Jones, C., & Spicer, A. (2009). *Unmasking the entrepreneur*. Cheltenham: Edward Elgar.
Kauppinen, A., & Juho, A. (2012). Internationalisation of SMEs from the perspective of social learning theory. *Journal of International Entrepreneurship, 10*(3), 200–231. http://link.springer.com/journal/volumesAndIssues/10843.
Kolb, D. A. (1984). *Experiential learning: Experience as the source of learning and development.* Englewood Cliffs, N.J.: Prentice-Hall.
Komarkova, I., Gagliardi, D., Conrads, J., & Collado, A. (2015). *Entrepreneurship competence: An overview of existing concepts, policies and initiatives*. Luxembourg: Publications Office of the European Union Retrieved from https://ec.europa.eu/jrc/en/institutes/ipts.
Kyrö, P. (2006). The transitional development of entrepreneurship-dialogue between new economic activity, work and freedom. *Estudios de Economia Aplicada, 24*(2).

Lackeus, M. (2015). Entrepreneurship in education. What, why, when, how. Entrepreneurship360. *Background paper*. Retrieved from http://www.oecd.org/cfe/leed/BGP_Entrepreneurship-in-Education.pdf.

Lave, J., & Wenger, E. (1991). *Situated learning: Legitimate peripheral participation*. New York: Cambridge University Press.

Mainela, T., Puhakka, V., & Servais, P. (2015). Boundary crossing for international opportunities. *Journal of International Entrepreneurship, 13*(3), 173–185.

Man, T. W. Y. (2006). Exploring the behavioural patterns of entrepreneurial learning: A competency approach. *Education & Training, 48*(5), 309–321.

Mezirow, J. (1997). Transformative learning: Theory to practice. *New directions for adult and continuing education, 1997*(74), 5–12.

Miettinen, R. (2000). The concept of experiential learning and John Dewey's theory of reflective thought and action. *International Journal of Lifelong Education, 19*(1), 54–72.

Minniti, M., & Bygrave, W. (2001). A dynamic model of entrepreneurial learning. *Entrepreneurship Theory and Practice, 25*(3), 5–16.

Morselli, D. (2017). How do Italian vocational teachers educate for a sense of initiative and entrepreneurship? Development and initial application of the SIE questionnaire. *Education+Training*.

Morselli, D., Costa, M., & Margiotta, U. (2014). Entrepreneurship education based on the change laboratory. *The International Journal of Management Education, 12*, 333–348.

Mwasalwiba, E. S. (2010). Entrepreneurship education: A review of its objectives, teaching methods, and impact indicators. *Education & Training, 52*(1), 20–47.

Neck, H. M., & Corbett, A. C. (2018). The scholarship of teaching and learning entrepreneurship. *Entrepreneurship Education and Pedagogy, 1*(1), 8–41.

OECD. (2010). *SMEs, entrepreneurship and innovation*. OECD Publishing Retrieved from http://dx.doi.org/10.1787/9789264080355-en.

OECD, & European Commission. (2013). *The missing entrepreneurs: Policies for inclusive entrepreneurship in Europe*. Paris: OECD.

Olaison, L., & Meier Sørensen, B. (2014). The abject of entrepreneurship: Failure, fiasco, fraud. *International Journal of Entrepreneurial Behavior & Research, 20*(2), 193–211.

Peltonen, K. (2015). How can teachers' entrepreneurial competences be developed? A collaborative learning perspective. *Education+Training, 57*(5), 492–511.

Penaluna, K., Penaluna, A., Usei, C., & Griffiths, D. (2015). Enterprise education needs enterprising educators: A case study on teacher training provision. *Education+Training, 57*(8/9), 948–963.

QAA. (2018). *Enterprise and entrepreneurship education: Guidance for UK higher education providers*. Gloucester: Quality Assurance Agency Retrieved from www.qaa.ac.uk.

Riese, H. (2010). Pedagogic entrepreneurship–an educational ideal for the school of the future? In J. Sjøvoll & K. Skogen (Eds.), *Creativity and innovation: Preconditions for entrepreneurial education* (pp. 79–90). Trondheim: Tapir Academic.

Ruskovaara, E., & Pihkala, T. (2013). Teachers implementing entrepreneurship education: Classroom practices. *Education+Training, 55*(2), 204–216.

Ruskovaara, E., & Pihkala, T. (2015). Entrepreneurship education in schools: Empirical evidence on the teacher's role. *The Journal of Educational Research, 108*(3), 236–249.

Sannino, A. (2011). Activity theory as an activist and interventionist theory. *Theory & Psychology, 21*(5), 571–597.

Sannino, A., Engestrom, Y., & Lahikainen, J. (2016). The dialectics of authoring expansive learning: Tracing the long tail of a change laboratory. *Journal of Workplace Learning, 28*(4), 245–262.

Sannino, A., Engestrom, Y., & Lemos, M. (2016). Formative interventions for expansive learning and transformative agency. *Journal of the Learning Sciences, 25*(4), 599–633.

Seikkula-Leino, J., Satuvuori, T., Ruskovaara, E., Hannula, H., & McCracken, M. (2015). How do Finnish teacher educators implement entrepreneurship education? *Education+Training, 57*(4).

Svedberg, G. (2010). *Pedagogical entrepreneurship in the formulation and realisation arena*. Trondheim: Tapir Academic.

Tedmanson, D., Essers, C., Dey, P., & Verduyn, K. (2015). An un common wealth… transforming the commons with purpose, for people and not for profit! *Journal of Management Inquiry, 24*(4), 439–444.
Valerio, A., Parton, B., & Robb, A. (2014). *Entrepreneurship education and training programs around the world: Dimensions for success*. Washington: World Bank.
van Woensel, C. (2008). *A toolkit for the European citizen. The implementation of key competences. Challenges and opportunities*. Brussels: Consortium of Institutions for Development and Research in Education in Europe.
Virkkunen, J., & Ahonen, H. (2011). Supporting expansive learning through theoretical-genetic reflection in the Change Laboratory. *Journal of Organizational Change Management, 24*(2), 229–243. https://doi.org/10.1108/09534811111119780.
Volkmann, C., Wilson, K. E., Mariotti, S., Rabuzzi, D., Vyakarnam, S., & Sepulveda, A. (2009). *Educating the next wave of entrepreneurs: Unlocking entrepreneurial capabilities to meet the global challenges of the 21st Century*.
Vozikis, G., Solomon, G., Winkel, D., Rideout, E. C., & Gray, D. O. (2013). Does entrepreneurship education really work? A review and methodological critique of the empirical literature on the effects of university-based entrepreneurship education. *Journal of Small Business Management*, (3), 329.
Wang, C. L., & Chugh, H. (2014). Entrepreneurial learning: Past research and future challenges. *International Journal of Management Reviews*, (1), 24.
Wenger, E. (1998). *Communities of practice: Learning, meaning, and identity.* New York: Cambridge University Press.

Open Access This chapter is licensed under the terms of the Creative Commons Attribution 4.0 International License (http://creativecommons.org/licenses/by/4.0/), which permits use, sharing, adaptation, distribution and reproduction in any medium or format, as long as you give appropriate credit to the original author(s) and the source, provide a link to the Creative Commons license and indicate if changes were made.

The images or other third party material in this chapter are included in the chapter's Creative Commons license, unless indicated otherwise in a credit line to the material. If material is not included in the chapter's Creative Commons license and your intended use is not permitted by statutory regulation or exceeds the permitted use, you will need to obtain permission directly from the copyright holder.

Chapter 2
The Assessment of Entrepreneurial Education

Abstract According to Biggs' theory of constructive alignment, when designing and delivering a course (not only of entrepreneurship) educators should consider a coherence between the learning outcomes, the teaching and learning activities and the assessment practices. Assessment in this context is defined as an educational practice serving to fill the gap between the desired outcomes and what the student has actually achieved; not only is assessment essential to promote learning in students, but also permits teachers to reflect on and enhance their programmes. This chapter concentrates on how to assess a sense of initiative and entrepreneurship (SIE) among students, in educational settings. It will do so by drawing on literature of key competences and entrepreneurial education. The key finding is that assessment cannot be a 'one size fits all' process, but should be tailored to the institution and environments, with the active collaboration of the stakeholders. The final part of the chapter shows three best practices of entrepreneurial education in Ohio with a focus on assessment and the development of the SIE questionnaire for the evaluation of the way teachers educate for a SIE.

Keywords Assessment · Entrepreneurial education
Sense of initiative and entrepreneurship · Key competences
Competence-based education

This chapter explores the relevant literature on assessment through three streams: the assessment of competence, the assessment of key competencies and the assessment of entrepreneurial education. Within this scope, assessment is different from evaluation; while the former implies the learner's appraisal, the latter refers to the appraisal of providers, training methods or educators. The first section presents competence assessment with a suggested switch from psychometric to edumetric approaches, and the second describes the assessment of key competencies. In both assessments of competence and key competencies, formative assessment ('for' learning) plays a key role. The third section continues with the assessment of entrepreneurial education at secondary and tertiary level, with the literature evidencing an existing gap in assessment practices especially at secondary level. In enterprise, education forms

© The Author(s) 2019

D. Morselli, *The Change Laboratory for Teacher Training in Entrepreneurship Education*, SpringerBriefs in Education,
https://doi.org/10.1007/978-3-030-02571-7_2

of assessment 'as' learning should take place, with students choosing their own objectives and later rating the extent to which they have met them.

To this end, the chapter shows examples of entrepreneurial education and its evaluation. The fourth section describes three effective entrepreneurial education practices in Ohio, which testify to how the spirit of entrepreneurship can be integrated into a vibrant and rural context. The three examples deal with an introductory course in entrepreneurship, a course in social entrepreneurship, and a module in grant writing. These cases are examples of 'through' approaches to entrepreneurial education, with a focus on summative and formative assessment practices. Moreover, the three examples highlight the possibility for students to choose the ideas and values they want to pursue towards an 'as' learning approach and developing their autonomy. The fifth paragraph describes the development of the SIE questionnaire to evaluate the extent with which secondary teachers educate and act with a sense of initiative and entrepreneurship (SIE). By showing the strengths and weaknesses of the teachers, the SIE allows for the establishment of a baseline for the study shown in this book, thus paving the way for a formative intervention that would make the teachers more entrepreneurial.

Although there is much confusion concerning the terminology (Lackeus, 2015), and it is sometimes difficult to set apart the different forms of education, this chapter tries to rely on the following definitions of entrepreneurship: (1) entrepreneurship education represents the functional view of entrepreneurship, that is venture creation, (2) enterprise education embeds a broad educational view of entrepreneurship, a proactive mindset to turn ideas into action useful in many contexts and in a lifelong learning perspective; (3) entrepreneurial education is the general unifying term for the other similar terms; (4) the key competence of initiative and entrepreneurship represents the outcome for enterprise education.

2.1 The Assessment in Competence-Based Education

The fact that the curriculum and its assessment have a strong relationship causes both benefits and drawbacks (European Commission, 2012). The disadvantages are that when only some of the subjects are assessed, the assessment restricts the focus of the school programme causing the omission of the subjects that are not assessed. Similarly, if only some aspects of a topic are assessed, the assessment alters the topic itself. When the teacher only assesses the knowledge related to a subject, the student learning of attitudes and skills is at best incidental. Since the link between knowledge, skills and attitudes is not linear nor uniform, the information concerning one component cannot be merely achieved by assessing another component as proxy (Pepper, 2011). However, the close relation between the curriculum and its assessment also brings advantages. It informs about what is important to be learnt, not only what can be assessed with ease. Moreover, the assessment can result in more effort and time being spent on what is negotiated by students and teachers as important in the curriculum. Assessment can also support a switch from what is taught in a topic to how it is taught; this change would imply a shift to the pedagogies being in line with a flexible approach to teaching and learning, which is essential to develop students' key competences.

Any assessment method distinguishes between the stimulus format and the response format. The former is the type of task given to the individual to be assessed; the latter is the way the response is collected. Research highlights that what is measured is more dependent on the stimulus format than the response format. Hence when designing an assessment, educators should pay more attention to the stimulus format (van der Vleuten, Sluijsmans, & Joosten-ten Brinke, 2017). Another distinction made in education is between formative and summative assessment. During a period of instruction, formative assessment (also known as 'for' learning) uses the information obtained to encourage the student's learning (European Commission, 2012) so that teachers and students know what learning is taking place. Formative assessment provides feedback essential for teaching, since the efficacy of teaching methods is related to the formative feedback they can provide. It is a meaningful teaching and learning activity that uses the recognition of error to correct it (Biggs & Tang, 2011). Since it is closely related to learning, it promotes the development of the key competence of learning to learn (European Commission, 2012). At the end of an instruction period, the summative assessment (also called 'of' learning) summarises the student's learning (European Commission, 2012). The outcomes are utilised to grade students, the aim being to determine how well learners have acquired what they were expected to learn (Biggs & Tang, 2011). Summative assessment can be internal or external. Internal means that the assessment is used by the educational institution for internal purposes, for example to inform teachers, students and parents. External summative assessment refers to the use of assessment, for example in reviewing accountability, recruitment or certification (European Commission, 2012). An assessment task can be used either formatively or summatively and both are needed; it is imperative, however, that the learner knows for which purpose it is being used (Biggs & Tang, 2011).

The following are strategies and tools particularly effective for formative assessment (van der Vleuten et al., 2017). Firstly, as students' self-directed learning is promoted by continuous reflection and feedback, effective feedback is the most powerful tool to turn an assessment into a formative assessment. Feedback is characterised by information given to the student to modify his or her thinking and behaviour with the aim to improve learning. Effective feedback involves two types of data: verification, a simple judgement whether the answer provided is right or wrong; and elaboration, a message providing useful data to lead the learner to the correct response. The consequence is that the teaching staff should be trained not just to be 'objective', but to give learners effective feedback. Second, self-assessment is another important assessment strategy: to become good learners in a lifelong learning perspective, students need to learn to keep up with the latest discoveries in the field and perform a variety of actions to promote their continuous improvement. The third instrument is peer-assessment defined as a process where groups of learners rate their peers. The fourth tool is rubrics with grids allowing teaching staff to have a coherence between levels of performance and criteria.

Within a position paper, Birenbaum et al. (2006) criticise the evaluation practices across Europe because they do not meet the demands posed by a knowledge society and economy. This document argued that assessment practices tend to concentrate on assessment 'of' learning instead of assessment 'for' learning. Summative assessment becomes unauthentic, uneconomical, inflexible, context independent, thus resulting in demotivation for teachers and students. By contrast, the assessment 'for' learning is flexible, embedded in the context, authentic, integrated into the curriculum and multidimensional. Since research has shown that there is no better impulse for learning than assessment, new methods are called for to assess how students develop their competence (Baartman, Bastiaens, Kirschner, & van der Vleuten, 2007). It is therefore necessary to switch from a 'testing culture' to an 'assessment culture', meaning to move from a psychometric approach, to an 'edumetric' approach of assessment (Baartman et al., 2007); the following paragraphs explain the differences between these approaches.

The testing culture is based on a behaviourist view of learning and instruction, with the learner being considered a passive receiver of knowledge, with the teacher being considered the source of knowledge. Assessment and instruction are separated up to the point that external experts design the assessment tools to be used by teachers. In a testing culture, summative assessment prevails and tends to favour the result over the process. Moreover, this form of assessment targets basic skills and is based on reproducing the contents of class lectures and books, thus resulting in the focus of pedagogy and student learning switching to 'teaching to the test'. The most common testing instrument is the choice-response format (matching items, true and false, multiple choices) administered with paper and pencil tasks. The test is taken in class with time limits, and without the help of tools or materials. Concerning the quality evaluation, the testing culture leans on psychometric models of interpretation, scoring and development of tests. It is often used during high-stakes tests, and it is led by the need of fairness and objectivity in testing. It calls for high standardisation levels with the aim of searching for stable personal traits.

By way of contrast, the assessment culture was born from the growing critiques made on the traditional testing methods, given the unauthentic nature of tests and a loss of trust in them as valid tools to quantify learning. Constructivist learning theories ground this culture, with the learning process considered actively constructed by the individual. The learner cooperates with the teacher and the other students and shares responsibility for the learning process with reflection and self-evaluation practices. The assessment criteria are developed—and shared with—the help of students. An assessment culture also calls for varied assessment forms which are often not as standardised as in the testing culture. Assessment is both formative and summative; the process, not only the product, is assessed. The goal that is cultivated by this culture is the development of competence in both teacher and student. Rather than a stable trait, competence is expected to develop in the learner over time.

A competence assessment programme combines element of both testing and assessment cultures. Baartman et al. (2007) suggest thinking of assessment as programmes; since competence is a multifaceted whole of knowledge, skills and attitudes, a variety of methods are necessary to grasp its essence. The combination of methods that are used comprises a balance of formative and summative forms; the assessment methods vary and are functional to the goals of the educational programme. In competence-based education, assessment is criterion-referenced rather than norm-referenced (Biggs & Tang, 2011). While in norm-referenced assessment the goal is comparing learners to each other, in criterion-referenced assessment the aim is deciding if the student is competent or not. Assessing competence always involves the judgement by an expert. The reliability of judgment is often dealt with in terms of consensus among experts (van der Vleuten et al., 2017). Moreover, a consistent finding in research is that regardless of which method is used to measure competence, the results are context bound. The consequence of this finding is that diverse contexts should be sampled to make a proper inference or judgement. Hence, to be reliable an assessment should involve all stakeholders, with a pool of assessors and observations from diverse contexts.

Basing on the detailed literature review, Baartman et al. (2007) found ten criteria for competence assessment programmes:

1. Authenticity: a competence assessment programme should mirror the competences needed in future working life.
2. Cognitive complexity: a competence assessment programme should comprise high cognitive skills.
3. Fairness: all the learners should have the chance to display their capacity and increase their potential.
4. Meaningfulness: a competence assessment programmes should be significant for both students and teachers.
5. Directness: assessors should be able to directly interpret the results of the assessment.
6. Transparency: a competence assessment programme should be intelligible to all learners.
7. Education consequences: the extent with which an assessment affects instruction and learning.
8. Reproducibility of decisions: the decision made on the student is performed by means of multiple assessments, with a variety of assessors on diverse occasions.
9. Comparability: a competence assessment programme should be the same for all participants, and the scoring should be consistent.
10. Cost and efficiency: the participants should find the assessment task feasible, and the investment in resources and time should be justified by the benefits for example in teaching and learning.

2.2 The Assessment of Key Competences

One of the educational issues around Europe is how to measure the attainment of key competencies. Evidence shows that what is effectively assessed in the curriculum is taken seriously and clarified by both learners and teachers (Halász & Michel,

2011). The challenge of assessing key competencies across the curriculum is confined to primary and secondary education, which are central to the European Reference Framework. The experience shows that the cross-curricular or transversal ethos of key competencies is not always perceived by educators, who tend to consider the first block of key competences as subject specific and neglect the second block (Pepper, 2011). The first four key competences are developed and assessed within their specific subjects, such as mother tongue, foreign languages, maths and science, and IT, while they are learned across a variety of contexts. By way of contrast, despite their relevance, the last four key competencies—that is learning to learn, social and civic competencies, SIE, cultural awareness and expression—are not generally associated within specific subjects. Consequently, they are rarely explicitly addressed.

When assessing key competences, there are two main challenges (Pepper, 2011). The first challenge is defining and 'unpacking' the learning outcomes, thus providing the basis for the assessment. Not only knowledge and skills, but also attitudes should be taken into consideration. Other factors to be considered are the application of key competences in diverse and authentic situations, and the thresholds at which specific competence levels are considered attained. The challenge is to provide enough details about the key competence that is going to be assessed without reducing the assessment to a series of procedural tasks or losing the cohesion of the key competence. Otherwise, the learners are at risk of not fully understanding the holistic dimension of the assessment. When learning outcomes are overly detailed the holistic nature is lost in favour of micro-tasks, and the assessment and the teaching and learning activities are expressed by pedantic long checklists of behaviours and actions (European Commission, 2012). Another issue to be considered is the aim of the assessment which should be negotiated among the various stakeholders. The second challenge is broadening the methodologies to gather information on the application of competences in diverse settings (Pepper, 2011). Such an assessment, not only able to access data on a wide range of aims and situations, but also capable of enhancing and reporting on their development, should be called 'assessment'.

Gordon et al. (2009) identified four assessment models of key competences across Europe: (1) cross-curricular subject, with key competences assessed explicitly; (2) cross-curricular subject assessed implicitly; (3) assessment of subject-specific competences; and (4) assessment of knowledge rather than competence. Model 1 and 2 place the most emphasis on cross-curricular competences encouraging holistic learning. Model 1 is used by countries like Belgium, France and Spain that established a set of transversal competences in the school curricula and developed the relative assessment. While the curriculum is still structured by areas or subjects, contexts are arranged within subjects and areas to enhance the key competences in a cross-curricular fashion. The assessment still concerns subjects and areas, but each transversal competence is explicitly assessed within the given subject or area. Model 2 features countries such as Denmark or Sweden which concentrate on enhancing knowledge, skills and sometimes attitudes in each area or subject across the school programme. These countries establish transversal constructs like skills, themes, objectives, and goals which are not an explicit target for assessment, yet are assessed by means of assessment based on the subject or area. In Model 3, countries such as Germany, Austria and Poland use a competence-based approach to deliver and assess the areas or subjects. However, rather than on transversal key competences, the focus of assessment, teaching and learning is on the competences pertaining to the subject or the area. Model 4 concerns countries such as Portugal and Greece, where the policy intention to reform the education system has been hindered by implementation issues, and knowledge rather than competence is still delivered and assessed. Table 2.1 reports the definitions of key terms: assessment, certification and validation.

The literature on validity can help the assessment of key competence as it provides an overarching criterion for the evaluation of the assessment (European Commission, 2012). An assessment validation starts with an unequivocal statement of the proposed answers and interpretation of the assessment results. With key competencies, the proposed interpretation can be the degree with which the learner has acquired the competences that "all individuals need for personal fulfilment and development, active citizenship, social inclusion and employment" (European Commission, 2007, p. 3). The broad idea of validity also embeds other criteria such as reliability, comparability, utility and equity (European Commission, 2012). Another aspect of validity is the purpose of assessment, which is either formative or summative. A test can be rendered more reliable by reducing its types of questions and formats of response, thus making it unequivocal for learners to answer and for assessors to interpret. By assessing a reduced quantity of behaviour and actions, a summative assessment strengthens reliability; while by assessing a wider range of performances in different contexts, the formative assessment strengthens the overall validity. Moreover, a vast array of methods as well as source and types of information are necessary to help students develop and display their key competences (European Commission, 2012). Although the recommendations above argue in favour of a constructivist approach over a transmissive approach for teaching, the constructivist approach is more resource-intensive especially for teachers and researchers; teachers need time to discuss, reflect and plan. However, a constructivist approach is more in line with student-centred approaches for the development of key competences (Morselli, 2018).

Table 2.1 Definitions of key terms: assessment, certification and validation

Assessment of learning outcomes: the process of appraising knowledge, know-how, skills and/or competences of an individual against predefined criteria (learning expectations, measurement of learning outcomes). Assessment is typically followed by certification
Certification of learning outcomes: process of issuing a certificate, diploma or title formally of learning outcomes attesting that a set of learning outcomes (knowledge, know-how, skills and/or competences) acquired by an individual have been assessed by a competent body against a predefined standard
Validation of learning outcomes: confirmation by a competent body that learning outcomes (knowledge, skills and/or competences) acquired by an individual in a formal, non-formal or informal setting have been assessed against predefined criteria and are compliant with the requirements of a validation standard. Validation typically leads to certification

Source European Commission, Cedefop, and ICF International, (2014, pp. 28, 43, 288)

Portfolios are an elective tool for the assessment of key competences in a vast array of domains (European Commission, 2012). Teachers should encourage students to gather the relevant evidence on the development of their key competencies across the curriculum. The assessment of portfolios should be performed basing on three elements: the purpose of assessment; the guidelines for the items to be selected; the assessment criteria of the content. Also for Pepper (2011), portfolios are a convenient tool for both formative and summative assessment and should represent a logical collection of the meaningful items produced by the learner. E-portfolios can be convenient to collect evidence on digital competencies; information can be gathered with videos, audios, pictures and texts. The use of ICT for assessment could speed up assessment with targeted and timely feedback, tracking of the advancement, and interactive learning with a simulation of authentic contexts.

2.3 The Assessment of Entrepreneurial Education

In the literature, there is a considerable gap concerning the assessment of entrepreneurial education (Pittaway & Edwards, 2012). This section reviews the few studies on the assessment of entrepreneurial education in secondary and tertiary education with a special focus on the UK, the country that produces most of the literature on entrepreneurship and enterprise education (Blenker, Trolle Elmholdt, Hedeboe Frederiksen, Korsgaard, & Wagner, 2014). Apart from the UK NFER guidelines described below, this paucity is even greater for secondary institutions, given the lack of support from the agencies that are responsible secondary education in UK, and the additional problem of how to assess entrepreneurial pedagogies (Draycott, Rae, & Vause, 2011).

Connected to assessment there is the issue of impact, which is defined as changes detected as a direct consequence of an educational activity at different levels. A review from the European Commission (2015) shows that entrepreneurial education is effective, and similar to any type of education, it has an impact that can be detected on diverse levels: the learner, the institution, the wider economy and society. In the literature review, Mwasalwiba (2010) focuses on studies that measure the impact on learners as a consequence of attending tertiary courses in entrepreneurship education. He finds that because of the selection of success indicators, the outcomes tend to be biased to favour the learning outcomes on entrepreneurship. New venture creation is the most important indicator of success, followed by the students' academic standards and changes in their perception: interest, attitudes, self-confidence, self-efficacy and skills towards entrepreneurship. However, if examined closely, most questions on attitudes concern the students' intention to open their own business, the major rationale of which is to make profit.

Pittaway and Edwards (2012) provide a review of assessment practices in entrepreneurial education at tertiary level. Although the programmes that are surveyed concern the making of profits rather than wider educational entrepreneurship, the methodology they apply helps shed light on the assessment practices especially in the USA and in UK. The authors' review includes roughly 120 programmes, of which three quarters are delivered in the USA, and only one fourth in UK. To understand assessment practice, researchers should have in mind the different forms that entrepreneurial education can take, since various forms have diverse learning outcomes and call for different assessment methods (Pittaway & Cope, 2007). Entrepreneurial programmes can be classified into four approaches (Gibb, 2002; Lackeus, 2015; Pittaway & Edwards, 2012): 'about', 'for', 'through' and 'embedded'. 'About' approaches are theoretical and guided by content, the aim being to present a general understanding of entrepreneurship. 'For' approaches are oriented to occupation and seek to provide budding entrepreneurs with the required skills and knowledge. 'Through' approaches are often experiential, the aim going through a real entrepreneurial learning process in 'safe' conditions. While 'for' and 'about' approaches are convenient for a subset of secondary and tertiary students whose intention is to become entrepreneurs, 'through' approaches are useful to all students at any educational level (Lackeus, 2015). In 'embedded' approaches, entrepreneurship is delivered within other non-business subjects, the rationale being to endow learners with entrepreneurial experience and awareness relevant for their field of study (Pittaway & Edwards, 2012).

The overwhelming majority of courses which Pittaway and Edwards (2012) inspect make use of 'about' forms, while only one-tenth utilised 'through' forms, and only 3% 'embedded forms'. A major implication of this finding is that most of the courses under review do not prepare the students for entrepreneurial activities. Instead, their aim is to provide knowledge and giving an understanding of entrepreneurship. In 60% of the cases, 'about' forms of entrepreneurship training are underpinned by learning outcomes such as knowledge and understanding. 'For' forms are equally divided into attainment of understanding and knowledge, as well as the development of skills and competences. 'Through' approaches concentrate on relationships, empathy and competences. The majority of assessment methods are business plans and reports, with presentations and in-class assessments being the second most common. The traditional methods by contrast—such as tests, exams and essays—are being used far less frequently. Apart from teachers, the stakeholders seldom have a voice in what the assessment is going to be about, and objective assessment methods prevail with the use of summative assessment methods.

Draycott and Rae (2011) analyse 10 different frameworks for enterprise education. Although these frameworks have in common that they all focus on the delivery of soft skills and on raising the awareness of what enterprise means in secondary education, they differ substantially and cause confusion among educators. Draycott and Rae also note that competence frameworks exemplify a corporate-bureaucratic attitude aiming at standardizing, prescribing and controlling what is learned and taught, and this standardizing attitude may thwart the flexibility, spontaneity and creativity that should characterise an entrepreneurial experience. Komarkova, Gagliardi, Conrads and Collado (2015) suggest that a variety of assessment methods is likely to be the appropriate approach in entrepreneurial education, including formative and summative methods, as well as self-assessment and project work. The assessment of innovation and creativity could be carried out via tasks asking learners to spot opportunities and challenging norms, and by being adaptable and flexible in situations entailing risks and ambiguity (QAA, 2012). Moreover, constructively aligned curricula should make use of the SOLO taxonomy, thus allowing for unintended learning outcomes entailing creativity (Biggs & Tang, 2011). Assessment of enterprise education has been sometimes performed through written business plans (QAA, 2012); while this form of assignment can be valuable, it is improbable that this tool can detect the whole range of entrepreneurial behaviours (Jones & Penaluna, 2013).

Draycott et al. (2011) suggest considering the following aspects when assessing enterprise education in schools: (1) what to assess, (2) where the learning comes from and (3) what are the available assessment forms. Concerning what to assess (1), it is challenging to assess learning outcomes because they are either too general or too specific. An alternative approach could be that the students decided the outcomes with guidance from the teaching staff. This radical approach called assessment 'as' learning is explained below. The source of learning (2) should also be considered: since entrepreneurial skills are transversal, they can be learnt in diverse contexts inside and outside the school. Such variety leads to the use of self-assessment tools which raises concerns on validity and reliability when used alone. Regarding the possible assessment forms (3), which can be 'of', 'for' or even 'as' learning. While 'of' and 'for' forms are the summative and formative assessment forms explained above in this chapter, the 'as' learning form is the most radical form of assessment and is probably the most characteristic of an entrepreneurial pedagogy. In this context, students take the lead of their learning and assessment processes; they are responsible for setting their own objectives, monitoring their progress and reflect on their performance. In line with 'as' assessment forms of learning, some authors (Jones, Matlay, Penaluna, & Penaluna, 2014; Penaluna & Penaluna, 2015) have suggested a progression model for assessment: from pedagogy, which is teacher-centred, to student-centred andragogy, where there is a certain degree of self-determination on the part of the learner, to student-led heutagogy, where the student is considered to be a self-determined, motivated and autonomous learner who seeks guidance and negotiates access to learning resources.

Returning to Draycott et al. (2011), there are five principles to be followed for the assessment of enterprise education:

- The underlying pedagogy should be flexible, thus enabling learners to choose the targets he or she wants to achieve.
- The learning outcomes should be meaningful and relevant for the learners.
- It should be possible to trace the assessment and consider what was acquired both within and outside the curriculum.
- Students should understand the rationale behind the assessment.
- A mix 'of', 'for' and 'as' assessment forms should be considered.

Moreover, the only guide on how to assess the outcomes for enterprise education specific for secondary schools has been produced by the UK National Foundation for Educational Research (Spielhofer & Lynch, 2008). The focus is on the students, but the entire institution is involved to define the assessment process and the learning outcomes. It is important to note that this process takes time to develop, and a school should consider embedding enterprise education across the whole curriculum for one year before carrying out the actual assessment. An assessment process should be prepared as follows:

- A clear definition of the learning outcomes should be agreed upon with teachers and students, thus ensuring the commitment of the participants for the development of their enterprising capability.
- The learning outcomes should be written so to consider a progression of achievement levels.
- The teaching staff should be made aware of the ways with which they already teach and assess enterprise education.
- Teachers should also learn other ways to teach and develop an enterprise capability across or beyond the curriculum, for example with extra-school activities.

Concerning the assessment itself, NFER (Spielhofer & Lynch, 2008) recommends considering three aspects: (1) the scope: to improve the students' enterprise capability or just to recognise it, to achieve a recognised qualification; (2) the specific learning outcomes to be assessed; (3) the tools for the assessment, they can be paper and pencil or IT based. The NFER guide also provides six possible examples of assessment. To summarise and turn into practice what has been discussed so far, the following two sections are dedicated to examples of evaluation and assessment. While the next paragraph shows three best practices in entrepreneurial education in terms of learning outcomes, teaching and learning activities and assessment practices, the fifth paragraph considers the features of the teacher educating with the aim of cultivating students' sense of initiative and entrepreneurial attitudes.

2.4 Examples of Best Practices in Entrepreneurial Education

As has been stated in the first chapter, America is the worldwide leader in entrepreneurship both for culture and education. This paragraph describes three best practices in entrepreneurial education the researcher could find during his Fulbright Research Scholarship at Ohio University: (1) a module in grant writing for 15 years' old high students engaged in general education; (2) a course in social entrepreneurship for Bachelor students; (3) an introductory course in entrepreneurship education for non-business Bachelor students. They are examples of "through" approaches to entrepreneurial education that is the creation of an enterprising mindset necessary for each citizen. When possible, the best practices will be described according to Biggs and Tang's (2011) theory in terms of learning outcomes, teaching and learning activities and assessment practices. It is noteworthy that not only are the best practices characterised by formative assessment, but the students have a degree of freedom in choosing the ideas they want to pursue, thus taking an andragogical approach and developing the students' autonomy.

2.4.1 Module on Grant Writing

This module aims to teach the students how to be a grant writer, with the aim of giving them the skills to tackle possible problems or needs affecting their community. The students learn to do so by presenting a grant proposal in groups, pitching it in front of judges—the local business owners. It is delivered in a southern High School in Ohio supported by the Voinovich School of Leadership and Social Affairs and is completed during roughly 15 teaching hours in three weeks. The module is delivered by the English Language Arts teacher who points out a problem that the local community or industry perceives as important, that the students can address. Firstly, the teacher liaises with the local industry to look for entrepreneurs who are willing to spend three hours in collaboration. One hour is for the initial meeting with the teacher to develop a real-life business problem scenario; the second hour is to visit the classroom and engage the students in solving a real business problem; and the last hour is to return to the classroom and give feedback on the students' creative, researched solutions. In exchange, the entrepreneur's business is featured on the school's website.

An example of a problem proposed by the Voinovich School is "What potential problem does this high school have that could be solved by applying for a small grant to a local foundation or donor?" Elements to be considered or defined in this problem-solution approach are the brainstorming of potential solutions, the search for local grant-providing agencies, the hunt for types of grants provided and the nature of expectations after being awarded, a good value for money idea. The teacher also takes care of the prerequisites for this module, and these are the basic abilities on essay writing, presentations and brainstorming.

The students are divided into groups of four, and by the end of the module, they produce two outcomes for each group. The first outcome is a presentation evaluated by external judges on the prototype of solution, and the students actually produce the idea to be shown to the entrepreneur. The second outcome is a paper that explains in a persuasive way why the idea is the best solution. Hence, the students work in groups and by projects. The students develop, as a team, a timeline of daily goals which they revisit and set at the beginning of each class meeting, so that students learn how to plan their activities and sharing the responsibilities in group work. During the module, an expert visits the school and lectures on the essentials of grant writing, including: the problem/solution equation, finding a funder, researching the funder's mission, the value proposition, the match between the proposal and the grantee, leveraging resources, the budget, as well as the impact and sustainability of the project's goals.

The assessment is completed alongside three activities: an in-class PowerPoint presentation of the proposal, essay on the proposal and quality of group work. These activities are assessed summatively through the use of rubrics, but are also assessed formatively through in-class coaching; for example by asking who is doing what and by checking the individuals' contributions on Google docs, or by giving feedback during the rehearsal of the presentation. For example, the rubrics for the assessment of teamwork features the following criteria: distribute tasks, collaborate and contribute equitability, manage conflict, effectively reflect on teamwork, build consensus, manage time, set goals, stay on task, come prepared, maintain positive attitude. The rubric for the assessment of the presentation has the following criteria: explanation of ideas, organisation, physicality, word usage and teamwork.

2.4.2 *Introductory Course in Entrepreneurship*

The introductory course in entrepreneurship is for Bachelor students of any faculty, although primarily for non-business students, and it has no particular prerequisites. It is delivered in 15 weeks, and its aims are (1) raising awareness and curiosity in entrepreneurship, (2) learning key terms and concepts, (3) practicing the process of idea generation and pitching. The course is then equally split into the "about" entrepreneurship with the acquisition of basic knowledge to raise one's awareness, and "through" approach, to learn the entrepreneurial process in an experiential way. The teaching and learning activities related to the "about" approach are delivered by means of interactive lectures and evaluated with multiple choice tests. In the quizzes, the student has to apply principles of entrepreneurship dealt with during the lectures to answer questions posed in hypothetical fact situations. An example of this form of questioning is the following:

> A group of radio stations operating in and around the city of Atlanta form a trade association to lobby against proposed new laws being considered by the state of Georgia which would hurt the stations' ability to operate profitably. What kind of relationship describes the radio operators' association? (a) Limited partnership, (b) cooperation, (c) buyer supplier, (d) joint-venture.

Concerning the "through" assessment approach, there are two activities that the students undertake. The first is carried out individually and consists of interviewing an entrepreneur and writing a report. The report states what the student found inspiring, but also the topics dealt with in the class which connect to the interview. The second task is team based and concerns the development of a business idea with a focus on the essentials of a new venture, for example the value proposition. This activity has diverse outcomes that reproduce the entrepreneurial learning process: an executive summary of the idea, a 3-minute elevator pitch to raise money with possible investors, a tradeshow with an orientation to the consumer, a YouTube video also pitching potential investors, and a final report summarising the key elements of a business plan that could be submitted to potential investors. These four outcomes are assessed both formatively with feedback to the groups and summatively with rubrics. Concerning the formative feedback, in the case of pitching students rehearse in front of the class and receive feedback both from their schoolmates and the teacher. In the case of the executive summary, the students receive written comments by the teacher which are also discussed during group coaching.

The rubric criteria for the elevator pitch are the following: (a) overall, with the group's understanding of the business idea and its value proposition; (b) preparation and presentation, with the assessment of the teamwork, their preparation and fluency during the presentation; (c) message or content, to assess how well the team conveys the opportunity for an investor, the market opportunity and size, competitive advantage and team qualifications; (d) engagement, to understand how well the presentation conveyed the teams' engagement and enthusiasm in the idea or opportunity. The assessment criteria for the trade show exhibits are (1) the quality of the trade stands with visual attractiveness and prototypes; (2) the engagement with public and judges with the way the team pitches the idea and explain the business, (3) the team understands its product or service, and (4) the team attracting friends and attendants. It is clear from the grading criteria that the focus is not on the viability of the business itself, but rather on the understanding of key parts of the business model and how well the idea is developed and presented. Examples of ideas include an on-campus bike rental service for students at Ohio University; the patenting of jewels which are embedded with technology that allows students to ask for help in case of danger; on-campus smoothie vending machines; the patenting of golf balls with a GPS core that allows for their retrieval.

2.4.3 Course in Social Entrepreneurship

The course in social entrepreneurship at the Voinovich School of Leadership and Social Affairs takes a non-profit sector orientation and embeds the instances of citizenship and active participation for the creation of value for the local community. In other words, it seeks to awaken a civic sense to contrast apathy and helplessness. The targets are Bachelor and Master students of any discipline, and there are no particulars prerequisites. The basic principle underpinning the course is that social issues such as poverty do not have efficient solutions. Rather, these phenomena have to be observed in their daily manifestations to be partially tackled concretely at the level of the local community. An example for this could be the lack of a supermarket in town. This forces the poor to shop in the only central venue, a fuel station, which however is missing fresh vegetables and fruits, thus leading to an impoverished diet.

Instead of seeing development as filling gaps, the approach aims at the development of the already present assets. Rather than searching for grants for solving the issues identified as important, which would open the issue of sustainability, it is better to look for the most convenient use of the already available resources. This attitude requires the activation of the individual who looks for enterprising opportunities for change. Social entrepreneurship is thus defined as convincing people about ideas that are worth pursuing, and this criterion is the driving force behind the rubric to grade the course participants.

The course lasts 12 weeks and has three main teaching and learning activities. While the first two activities are carried out individually and aim to make emerge the student's values and orientations towards social entrepreneurship, the third activity is performed in groups and concerns the application of value and orientations to concrete problems affecting the local community. The first activity is called the "about me" assignment. Using a picture of him or herself and in whatever media desired, the student has to convey to the teacher who they are: what they do, what they like, and their aspirations. The second assignment entails reading a book on social entrepreneurship. In a sort of pitch, the student has five minutes to present the content to their schoolmates; the focus on the lesson learnt, why they liked (or disliked) it, and why it would be worth reading. The last activity is a project on the collective co-creation of value. The teacher starts by telling motivating stories from around the world of problems that have been tackled by making the best use of available resources. The group has first to spot something that could be tackled in their community and then elaborate a plan about how to use the resources that could be marshalled to solve it. The final product is a presentation that has to be as convincing as possible from the teacher and expert's perspective.

2.5 The Characteristics of Entrepreneurial Teachers, Assessing the Way They Educate for a Sense of Initiative and Entrepreneurship. The SIE Questionnaire

The SIE questionnaire seeks to measure how secondary teachers educate for the key competence of the SIE as cross-curricular subject. Any teacher could therefore teach for a SIE while teaching their subject. One possible way to do that is to teach in an entrepreneurial way, thus becoming a role model for their students (European Commission, 2014; Penaluna, Penaluna, Usei, & Griffiths, 2015). Based on an extensive literature review, Morselli (2017) evidenced five characteristics of the entrepreneurial teacher:

The first feature is embedding the SIE learning outcomes and student-centred assessment practices within the teaching of a subject. Learning outcomes need to be delivered horizontally, across the curriculum, and vertically, to ensure progression through all levels of compulsory education (European Commission, EACEA, & Eurydice, 2016). It is maintained that coherence should be sought between learning outcomes, teaching and learning activities and assessment as suggested by the theory of constructive alignment (Biggs & Tang, 2011). Learning outcomes should be a balanced mix of knowledge, skills and attitudes and should not be so fragmented as to lose the holistic nature of the key competence (Pepper, 2011). Teachers should consider using a variety of assessment forms: 'of' learning, 'for' learning and 'as' learning. Assessment could move progressively from pedagogy to andragogy and to heutagogy, with students selecting the goals they want to achieve and self-assessing the extent with which they have been met.

The second feature of teachers undertaking cross-curricular education for a SIE is a focus on active teaching, for example experiential learning, group work, project work, problem-solving and mentoring. These can be combined or varied according to the subject taught.

The third feature is educating for entrepreneurial attitudes. Active teaching should aim at developing an entrepreneurial mindset with attitudes such as creativity, risk-taking, autonomy and responsibility in the individual depending on their progress.

The fourth feature of teachers undertaking cross-curricular education for a SIE is networking activities between and between school and work. Partnerships can be both within schools with other colleagues, subjects and courses, and outside the school, to engage students in meaningful activities and avoid the 'encapsulation' of knowledge acquired at school. In vocational subjects, teachers having a working relationship with the industry connected to the vocation or subject taught are regarded in a positive light, as the teacher has up-to-date competencies and knows the needs of industry, and can therefore plan activities for students that cross the boundaries of the school, the course and the subject.

The fifth feature is seeing entrepreneurialism as a lifelong learning pursuit, namely inside and outside the school context and throughout professional development. The entrepreneurial teacher participates in specific courses on entrepreneurship but also in broader ways develops his or her own SIE, for example through new ideas for promoting creativity, risk-taking, autonomy and responsibility. Discussion about pedagogical entrepreneurship with other teaching staff and colleagues is also a good indicator of the extent to which the topic is felt to be important in the school.

These five dimensions are used in the SIE questionnaire and adapted for the specific environment that is an Italian vocational secondary education teachers and workshop assistants. Table 2.2 shows the content of the SIE questionnaire.

The questionnaire has been administered to 21 teachers facilitating the courses of surveying and logistics, of which 10 are technical teachers, seven are workshop assistants and four are humanities and science teachers. Table 2.3 shows the results.

From the results, it could be argued that teaching staff educate for different aspects of the SIE. For example, although technical teachers teach mostly by means of lectures, they are the most entrepreneurial in life, and the individuals to cross the boundary between school and work the most with a second job in industry. Not surprisingly, workshop assistants are the most willing to use active didactics: learning by doing, mentoring and project work; they also are the most entrepreneurial inside the school. Concerning humanities and science teachers, they are the only ones who go sometimes beyond assessment 'of' learning, as they prefer to use assessment 'for' and 'as' learning.

The use of the SIE questionnaire displays the strengths and weaknesses of the teaching staff. The strengths of this group are that they see value in educating students for responsibility and autonomy, and to some extent embed in their teaching active didactics like mentoring and problem-solving. Furthermore, they are entrepreneurial in life and in the school environment. However, the results also show weaknesses and issues that should be dealt with in order to enhance the way teachers deliver a SIE as cross-curricular subject. The most significant drawback evidenced by the results is that the teachers use lectures as main didactics with corresponding assessment forms 'of' learning which tend to turn learners into passive receivers. The teachers' attention is geared towards the product and immediate concrete goals rather than on the process with educational aims in a lifelong learning perspective. This can be seen a 'teaching

Table 2.2 Five dimensions of the SIE developed into a questionnaire

Entrepreneurial learning outcomes, and 'as' and 'for' assessment forms
1. The sense of initiative and entrepreneurship has been a goal of my curriculum
2. I have assessed the sense of initiative and entrepreneurship of my students
3. I have developed assessments where the student chose their objectives and later self-evaluate their performance
Active entrepreneurial teaching
4. What is the percentage of your teaching you generally deliver through lectures?
5. I have organised practical experiences through learning by doing
6. I have organised class activities according to group work (e.g. cooperative learning)
7. I have organised in class activities according to project work
8. I have organised didactics based on problem-solving
9. I have utilised mentoring (e.g. by going to the students' seats and giving them advice on their work)
10. I have organised discussions to transform the classroom in a place of debate
Educating for entrepreneurial attitudes
11. I have taught my students how to deal with the risk connected with to be entrepreneurial, and learnt how to accept failure
12. I have sustained my students' initiative, for example by accepting their proposals
13. I have prepared activities where the students could express creativity and innovation
14. I have encouraged my students to take responsibilities and to be autonomous
Networking activities
15. I have established partnerships with industry/the outside world
16. I have involved experts during in-class lessons
17. I have organised school visits to places of interest
18. I have organised interdisciplinary projects with my colleagues
19. I work outside the school for the local industry
Being entrepreneurial as a lifelong learning pursuit, professional development
20. I have taken part in endeavours or courses stimulating my own sense of initiative and entrepreneurship
21. I have discussed entrepreneurial education with colleagues and experts
22. During my school life (in class and in the school), I show my sense of initiative and entrepreneurship
23. In my life outside the school, I show my sense of initiative and entrepreneurship

to the test', that is teaching for knowledge instead of competence. Although most vocational teachers have a second job in the vocation they have also been trained in, they seldom cross the boundaries between their school and other forms of work, by way of initiating interdisciplinary project, partnerships and inviting experts to school to lecture. Furthermore, the participants seldom participate in training that develops their SIE and never discussed the possibility of implementing entrepreneurship with their colleagues.

From CHAT point of view, the three entrepreneurial education *best practices* are examples of 'linear interventions' (see Engeström & Sannino, 2010) with a clear starting point, objectives, and with the students expected to participate in the intervention with no resistance. Part of the success of these courses depends on the fact

Table 2.3 Outcomes of the SIE questionnaire $N = 21$)

Area	Question	Average $N = 21$	Technical teachers $N = 10$	Workshop assistants $N = 7$	Humanities and science $N = 4$
Entrepreneurial learning outcomes, and 'as' and 'for' assessment forms	Goal of the curriculum	1	1	1	1
	Evaluation of key comp	1	1	1	1
	Evaluation 'for' and 'as'	1	1	1	2
Active entrepreneurial teaching	Lecture	50%	60%	40%	50%
	Learning by doing	2	2	4	2.5
	Group work	2	2	2	3
	Project work	2	2	3	1,5
	Problem-solving	3	3	2	2,5
	Mentoring	3	2,5	4	3
	Negotiation– debate	2	2	2	2.5
Educating for entrepreneurial attitudes	Risk management	1	1.5	1	1.5
	Initiative	2	2	2	3.5
	Creativity and innovation	2	2	2	2
	Responsibility and autonomy	3	3	3	3
Networking activities	Partnerships with industry	2	2	1	1,5
	Involvement of experts	1	1	1	1
	Company visits	2	2	2	1.5
	Interdisciplinary projects	1	1	2	1.5
	Second job in industry	Yes	Yes	No	No
Being entrepreneurial as a lifelong learning pursuit, professional development	Courses and initiatives on entrepreneurship	2	1.5	1	2.5
	Discussion with colleagues	1	1	1	1.5
	Entrepreneurship in school	3	2	3	2.5
	Entrepreneurship in life	3	3	3	2

Legend
Medians: 1 = Never; 2 = Sometimes; 3 = Often; 4 = Always

that they were delivered in America which is considered the most entrepreneurial friendly environment. The use of the SIE questionnaire, however, can be useful to establish a baseline for a formative intervention to support a change process. Such intervention could lead to the generation of an *emerging practice* with pedagogical renewal, thus making the teaching staff more entrepreneurial. Moreover, if repeated throughout the years, such *emerging practice could become the new costumeray way to do things, a best practice,* thus showing a possible circularity between formative and linear interventions. The next chapter explains the difference between formative and linear interventions and shows the theoretical underpinnings of the Change Laboratory to foster expansive learning.

Bibliography

Baartman, L. K., Bastiaens, T. J., Kirschner, P. A., & van der Vleuten, C. P. (2007). Evaluating assessment quality in competence-based education: A qualitative comparison of two frameworks. *Educational Research Review, 2*(2), 114–129.

Biggs, J., & Tang, C. (2011). *Teaching for quality learning at university. What the student does*. New York: McGraw-Hill.

Birenbaum, M., Breuer, K., Cascallar, E., Dochy, F., Dori, Y., Ridgway, J., … Nickmans, G. (2006). A learning integrated assessment system. *Educational Research Review, 1*(1), 61–67.

Blenker, P., Trolle Elmholdt, S., Hedeboe Frederiksen, S., Korsgaard, S., & Wagner, K. (2014). Methods in entrepreneurship education research: A review and integrative framework. *Education + Training, 56*(8/9), 697–715.

Draycott, M. C., & Rae, D. (2011). Enterprise education in schools and the role of competency frameworks. *International Journal of Entrepreneurial Behavior & Research, 17*(2), 127–145.

Draycott, M. C., Rae, D., & Vause, K. (2011). The assessment of enterprise education in the secondary education sector: A new approach? *Education & Training, 53*(8–9), 673–691.

Engeström, Y., & Sannino, A. (2010). Studies of expansive learning: Foundations, findings and future challenges. *Educational Research Review, 5*(1), 1–24.

European Commission. (2007). *European competences for lifelong learning*. Luxembourg: Publication Office of the European Union.

European Commission. (2012). *Thematic Working Group 'Assessment of Key Competences'. Literature review, glossary and examples*. Retrieved from http://ec.europa.eu/dgs/education_culture/repository/education/policy/school/doc/keyreview_en.pdf.

European Commission. (2014). *Entrepreneurship education. A guide for teachers*. Brussels: Unit Entrepreneurship 2020.

European Commission. (2015). *Entrepreneurship education: A road to success*. Brussels: Publication Office of the European Union.

European Commission, Cedefop, & ICF International. (2014). *European inventory on validation of non-formal and informal learning. Executive summary*. Luxemburg: Publication Office of the European Union.

European Commission, EACEA, & Eurydice. (2016). *Entrepreneurship education at school in Europe. Eurydice report*. Luxembourg: Publication Office of the European Union.

Gibb, A. (2002). In pursuit of a new 'enterprise' and 'entrepreneurship' paradigm for learning: Creative destruction, new values, new ways of doing things and new combinations of knowledge. *International Journal of Management Reviews, 4*(3), 233–269.

Gordon, J., Halász, G., Krawczyk, M., Leney, T., Michel, A., Pepper, D., … Wiśniewski, J. (2009). *Key competences in Europe: Opening doors for lifelong learners across the school curriculum and teacher education*. In Retrieved from http://www.case-research.eu/en/key-competences-in-europe-opening-doors-for-lifelong-learners-across-the-school-curriculum.

Halász, G., & Michel, A. (2011). Key competences in Europe: Interpretation, policy formulation and implementation. *European Journal of Education, 46*(3), 289–306.

Jones, C., Matlay, H., Penaluna, K., & Penaluna, A. (2014). Claiming the future of enterprise education. *Education + Training, 56*(8/9), 764–775.

Jones, C., & Penaluna, A. (2013). Moving beyond the business plan in enterprise education. *Education + Training, 55*(8/9), 804–814. https://doi.org/10.1108/et-06-2013-0077.

Komarkova, I., Gagliardi, D., Conrads, J., & Collado, A. (2015). *Entrepreneurship competence: An overview of existing concepts, policies and initiatives*. Luxembourg: Publications Office of the European Union. Retrieved from https://ec.europa.eu/jrc/en/institutes/ipts.

Lackeus, M. (2015). Entrepreneurship in Education. *What, why, when, how*. Retrieved from http://www.oecd.org/cfe/leed/BGP_Entrepreneurship-in-Education.pdf.

Morselli, D. (2017). How do Italian vocational teachers educate for a sense of initiative and entrepreneurship? Development and initial application of the SIE questionnaire. *Education + Training*.

Morselli, D. (2018). Teaching a sense of initiative and entrepreneurship with constructive alignment in tertiary non-business contexts. *Education + Training*.

Mwasalwiba, E. S. (2010). Entrepreneurship education: A review of its objectives, teaching methods, and impact Indicators. *Education + Training, 52*(1), 20–47.

Penaluna, K., Penaluna, A., Usei, C., & Griffiths, D. (2015). Enterprise education needs enterprising educators: A case study on teacher training provision. *Education + Training, 57*(8/9), 948–963.

Penaluna, A., & Penaluna, K. (2015). Thematic paper on entrepreneurial education in practice. Part 2. *Building motivation and competencies*. Retrieved from http://www.oecd.org/cfe/leed/Entrepreneurial-Education-Practice-pt2.pdf.

Pepper, D. (2011). Assessing key competences across the curriculum—And Europe. *European Journal of Education, 46*(3), 335–353.

Pittaway, L., & Cope, J. (2007). Simulating entrepreneurial learning integrating experiential and collaborative approaches to learning. *Management Learning, 38*(2), 211–233.

Pittaway, L., & Edwards, C. (2012). Assessment: Examining practice in entrepreneurship education. *Education + Training, 54*(8/9), 778–800.

QAA. (2012). *Enterprise and entrepreneurship education: Guidance for UK higher education providers*. Retrieved from http://www.qaa.ac.uk/en/Publications/Documents/enterprise-entrepreneurship-guidance.pdf.

Spielhofer, T., & Lynch, S. (2008). *Assessing enterprise capability: Guidance for schools*. Slough: National Foundation for Educational Research.

van der Vleuten, C., Sluijsmans, D., & Joosten-ten Brinke, D. (2017). Competence assessment as learner support in education. In M. Mulder (Ed.), *Competence-based vocational and professional education* (pp. 607–630). Switzerland: Springer.

Open Access This chapter is licensed under the terms of the Creative Commons Attribution 4.0 International License (http://creativecommons.org/licenses/by/4.0/), which permits use, sharing, adaptation, distribution and reproduction in any medium or format, as long as you give appropriate credit to the original author(s) and the source, provide a link to the Creative Commons license and indicate if changes were made.

The images or other third party material in this chapter are included in the chapter's Creative Commons license, unless indicated otherwise in a credit line to the material. If material is not included in the chapter's Creative Commons license and your intended use is not permitted by statutory regulation or exceeds the permitted use, you will need to obtain permission directly from the copyright holder.

Chapter 3
The Change Laboratory in Theory

Abstract This methodological chapter gives the reader an overview on Cultural-Historical Activity Theory, the theoretical framework used in the study, with expansive learning, a learning theory specific for collectiveness, innovation and change of social practices. Formative interventions, especially the Change Laboratory workshops, are designed to trigger cycles of expansive learning and are based on two principles, 'double stimulation' and 'ascending from the abstract to the concrete'. The interactions during Change Laboratory workshops can be recorded for later analysis, thus allowing the study of expansive learning as concept formation and development of collective transformative agency. This chapter also outlines how to organize and conduct a Change Laboratory within an organisation and the various tasks that can be used to promote expansive learning actions. While Cultural-Historical Activity Theory is broad, disputed and multifaceted, this chapter is based on the research of Engeström, Sannino and Virkkunen because they provide the theoretical foundation upon which to conduct an effective Change Laboratory.

Keywords Cultural-Historical Activity Theory · Expansive learning
Change Laboratory · Concept formation · Collective transformative agency

The chapter starts by introducing the three generations of Cultural-Historical Activity Theory (CHAT) from the Russian school of Vygotsky and Leon'tev, before moving to the contributions of more recent theorists such as Engeström. CHAT enlarges the focus of analysis to a collective activity system mediated by artefacts and oriented to an object. This activity system is studied in its network of relationships with the other connected activity systems for the purpose of studying expansive learning transformations for innovation and change of practices.

The second section presents formative interventions developed within the Vygotskian activist and interventionist legacy, which seeks to bring about cycles of expansive learning. It distinguishes between common variable-centred linear interventions from process-centred formative interventions useful to trigger expansive learning. The section also outlines the Change Laboratory, a type of formative intervention characterised by a highly mediated setting with writing surfaces used according to different levels of abstraction and to a historical perspective. The Change Laboratory

© The Author(s) 2019

D. Morselli, *The Change Laboratory for Teacher Training in Entrepreneurship Education*, SpringerBriefs in Education,
https://doi.org/10.1007/978-3-030-02571-7_3

also features an interplay between distanced intellectual analysis and close emotional involvement, by utilising mirrors such as video-taped materials gathered on the field that are later used to trigger discussion.

The following sections show the basic principles that formative interventions are based on. The third section explains the principle of double stimulation, which is thought of as the foundation of human will and the gateway to higher psychological functions. Double stimulation allows the development of collective transformative agency, when the participants break away from the given frame of action to implement a new model. A dialectical view of development characterises expansive learning with a thinking that differs substantially from common patterns of thought, and the fourth section presents the principle of ascending from the abstract to the concrete, that is the dialectical process of constructing theoretical concepts. Theoretical generalisations aim to arrive at the internal relationships of objects and their historical development. The fifth section explains how to prepare a Change Laboratory, including negotiating the intervention with the representatives, carrying out field research, scheduling and preparing the workshops. The sixth section gives an idea about the forms of tasks needed to engage the participants in the diverse expansive learning actions, including historical analysis and actual empirical analysis useful to promote theoretical generalisations.

The aim of this chapter is not to make a literature review of Change Laboratory, nor to enrich the theory with personal reflections. The goal is rather to explain the concepts that are important to frame this research and show that the Change Laboratory is a rigorous although flexible model with strong theoretical underpinnings. The basis is the manual of Virkkunen and Newnham (2013) which the reader is forwarded to consult for more complete information. The scholarship that underpins this chapter includes the work of Engeström and Virkkunen, the two authors who designed the Change Laboratory. The work of Sannino will also be reviewed as it is pivotal in forming a definition of a collective transformative agency.

3.1 Expansive Learning

Cultural-Historical Activity Theory (CHAT) is a theoretical framework that helps study and understand the relations between the human mind, with what individuals feel and think, their activity, as well as what individuals do (Daniels, 2016). Its origins come from the cultural-historical school of the Russian psychology. According to CHAT, the interaction between humans and other humans or with the environment is not fixed or determined by biology, but is mediated by tools (Virkkunen & Newnham, 2013). Engeström (1987) identified three generations of Activity Theory. The first generation was pioneered by Vygotsky, who first described the concept of mediation as a triadic relationship between the stimulus, the response and a complex act mediated by artefacts (Vygotsky, 1978, in Engeström, 2015). The idea of mediation in human action was revolutionary as it transcended the dualistic relationship between the individual and the society (Engeström, 2015). Thus, while the individual had to be considered in the light of his or her cultural means, the society had to be considered with regard to the individual who produces and make use of artefacts to interact with the world. With a switch from studying isolated elements to studying relationships, Vygotsky also redefined the scope of analysis to focus on units (Virkkunen & Newnham, 2013). A unit is the smallest combination of internal relations with a unity of opposites which still shows the dynamism and the qualities of the whole. The focus of the analysis, however, remained still centred on the individual (Engeström, 2015).

The second generation of CHAT was initiated by Leont'ev (1981, in Engeström, 2015) who thought of human activity as collective phenomenon oriented to an object. The activity is carried out by individuals through actions and operations. The main feature of an action is that it is consciously oriented to a goal in a specific time and place. Actions are made of and performed by means of routinised operations, which are carried out with automatic unconscious processes. The visualisation of human activity and its internal relationships with a triangular model has been proposed by Engeström (2015, p. 63). Figure 3.1 shows the triangular model of human activity.

Leont'ev also added the division of labour into the basic unit of analysis (Engeström, 2009). An activity can only be performed by breaking down jobs among the community members and appointing the diverse actions to the different participants. This definition implies rules coordinate interactions. Furthermore, for Leont'ev (1978, in Virkkunen & Newnham, 2013), the division of labour mediates between the social meaning of an activity and the meaning made by its members. While community members carry out short-lived and goal-oriented actions, activity system is enduring and object-oriented. Human motives cannot be traced in the individual's biology and materialise in collective human activities during the appropriation, use

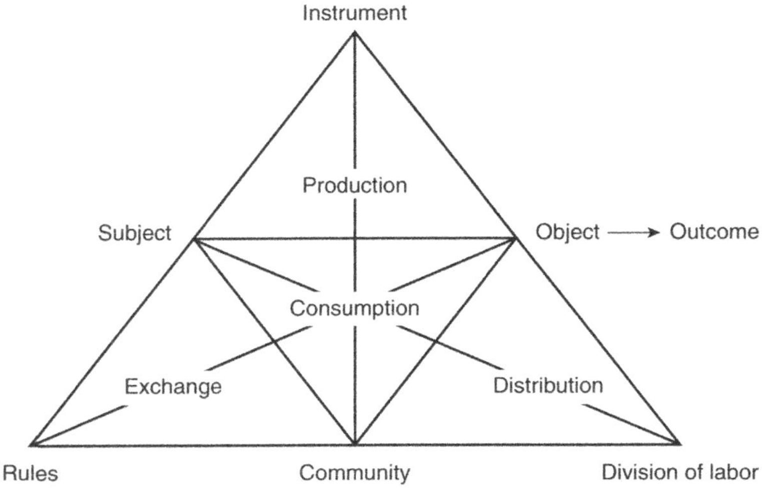

Fig. 3.1 Triangular model of human activity (Engeström, 2015, p. 63, reproduced with permission from Cambridge University Press)

and development of artefacts and objects (Miettinen, 2005). In an activity system, the object plays a key role, as it is the object which provides for the social meaning of the activity. The object, however, should not be confused with common definitions of 'object' or 'objective' (Virkkunen & Newnham, 2013). One example cited by Engeström (1990) is how a blacksmith makes use of the hammer to shape a chunk of iron. The blacksmith is the subject, the hammer is the instrument, and the piece of iron is the object. At one moment, the chunk of iron has no shape, but later it is a recognisable entity with a social meaning: the object is therefore contemporaneously given, projected and anticipated. This dual feature, abstract and concrete at the same time, shows the temporal and processual essence of objects, which crystallise and embody a historically accumulated collective experience. Furthermore, a shapeless mineral becomes the object of our action when we act on, perceive it, make hypotheses about it and imagine it. In doing so, the object becomes the motive and purpose of the action.

Starting from the 1980s, the third generation of CHAT has developed instruments to study networks of interacting activity systems, multiple perspectives and dialogue (Engeström, 2015). The focus is on communities seen as learners, creation and transformation of culture, hybridisation and horizontal movement and formation of theoretical concepts (Engeström & Sannino, 2010). In its present conceptualisation, CHAT can be summarised with the help of five principles (Engeström, 2000). The first principle is that the unit of analysis is a collective activity system mediated by artefacts and oriented to the object; an activity system of this type is considered in constantly evolving relationship with the other activity systems. The second tenet pertains to multi-voicedness; activity systems always embed a community with diverse points of view, interests and traditions due to the stories of individuals and their roles in the activity. The third principle contends that activity systems are born and transformed over long periods; consequently, their potentials and issues can be better grasped by taking an historical perspective. The fourth principle emphasises the role of contradictions as sources of development and change. Contradictions are different from simple conflicts or problems; they are historically accumulated structural tensions within and between activity systems. The fifth tenet suggests that there is always the possibility for expansive transformations. When the contradictions of an activity system become aggravated, some members start questioning and diverging from the established norms. They engage in a collective and purposeful effort to innovate and change. As a result, the practitioners achieve an expansive transformation when they succeed in reconceptualising the motive and the object of their activity so that there is a larger array of possibilities than in the previous activity system. Ideally, a cycle of expansive learning is composed of seven learning actions which logically follow from one another (Engeström, 2015), as displayed by Fig. 3.2.

The actions are (Engeström & Sannino, 2010; Virkkunen & Newnham, 2013):

1. To question, criticise or reject aspects of the current practices or present wisdom.
2. To analyse the situation with 'why' questions and explanations. The internal contradictions are found with a twofold analysis: an historical analysis of the changes occurred in the structure of the activity, and an actual empirical analysis

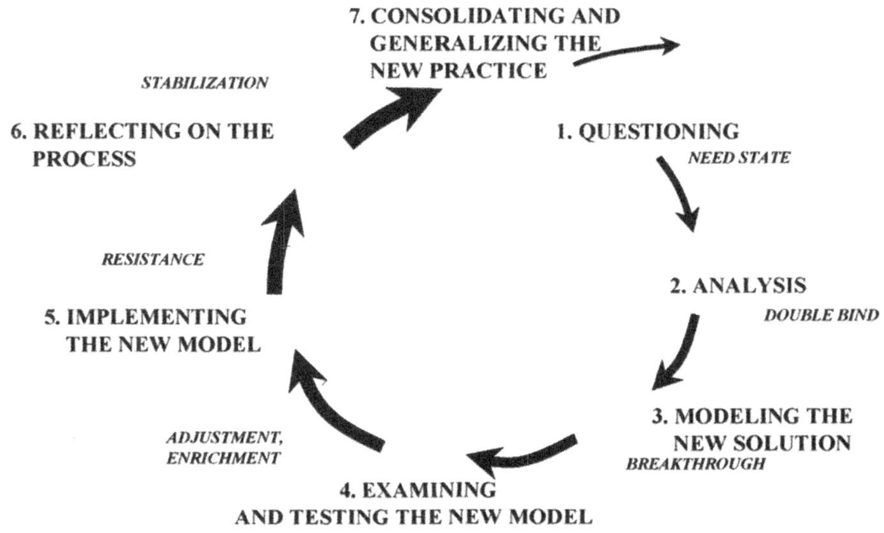

Fig. 3.2 Cycle of expansive learning (Engeström, 1999, p. 384). Reproduced with permission from Cambridge University Press

of the manifestations of contradictions in both daily practices and coordination among practitioners.
3. To model the new explanatory relationship in a way that can be observed and transmitted to the other members of the activity. This implies designing a germ cell, a simplified and explicit model of the novel idea.
4. To examine the new model and experiment it to evaluate its limitations, potentials and functioning.
5. To Implement the model in practice and enrich it.
6. To reflect on the model and evaluate the expansive learning process. The aim is to summarise the learning occurred during the process and look for further learning needs.
7. To consolidate the model into a stabilised practice and generalise it to other organisations or working units within the same organisation.

As stated by the fifth tenet above, contradictions play a significant role in expansive learning. In a market economy, each element of an activity (represented in Fig. 3.1) is part of two diverse systems of relationships that determine its features (Virkkunen & Newnham, 2013): (1) a specific function in the activity system, therefore connoting a use value; (2) a price in the market, therefore indicating an exchange value. This relationship between use value and exchange value causes a tension, yet each historical form of activity is a temporary way to manage such tension. The contrast between the two highlights the primary contradiction. The balance between use value and exchange value is strained when major changes occur in the elements and structure of the activity, or in the needs that the activity system fulfils, or in the market. Such strain transforms primary contradictions into secondary contradictions between some of the activity system components, which leads to antithetical requests to the practitioners. A change in the object, for example, could call for doing something that would be impossible to achieve with the present rules or instruments. A reconfiguration of the object and re-equilibrated activity system would then lead to tertiary contradictions between the existing form and the new model of the activity system implemented. Eventually, quaternary contradictions emerge between the fully transformed activity system and the network of related activity systems it depends on.

It is rare that the internal contradictions of an activity system manifest themselves directly rather they are arrived at through an interplay of two types of analysis. These complementary analyses characterise the second expansive learning action of Fig. 3.2: the historical analysis considers the transformation of the activity structure, while the actual empirical analysis inquiries about the actions that practitioners carry out every day (Virkkunen & Newnham, 2013). Contradictions can visibly manifest in deviations from scripts, waste in the process, ruptures, disturbances, conflicts and disagreements between individuals, but also practitioners' dilemmas, conflicts of motives, double binds. Table 3.1 outlines three key concepts related to contradictions: script, disturbance and rupture.

A large-scale cycle of expansive learning develops over years and solves the four types of contradictions towards a stable, radically new activity and system of relationships with the network of related activities. A large-scale cycle implies medium cycles, which are themselves formed by small cycles that could occur in a couple of hours. However, a small cycle could only be regarded as potentially expansive depending on the large-scale expansive transformation (Engeström, 2015). Expansive learning leads to a rediscovery of the activity: what the purpose is, what it is, who it serves. Such rediscovery is an empowering experience for the practitioners.

Schools have been often targeted by studies on expansive learning. Engeström (2009) suggests that studying learning environments as activity systems would help think the implementation of new technologies as an expansive learning process. While we consider technologies as universal and applicable in many settings, that is empirical generalisations, this interpretation tends to hide the cultural and historical specificity of the activity system where the technology is applied. Ignoring the speci-

Table 3.1 Terms related to contradictions

Script. Habitual, tacitly expected order of interacting participants' actions and the operations through which the actions are carried out
Disturbance. Negative deviation from the script or plan that puts the successful accomplishment of a collaborative work at risk
Rupture. When carrying out the script or plan or in the related communication, a rupture is a misunderstanding or failure to give or receive information that is pertinent to the process or to carry out a necessary action or operation. A rupture in communication often later leads to a disturbance

Source Virkkunen and Newnham (2013, p. 88)

ficities often results in problems, with practitioners resisting to the implementation. By contrast, if the activity system is taken as starting point "implementation no more appears a task of implanting an alien bubble in an unknown territory" (p. 25).

3.2 Formative Interventions

Activity Theory comes from a longstanding interventionist and activist tradition that scholars such as Vygotsky, Leont'ev and Luria (Sannino, 2011) developed during the historical turmoil of Russia. This tradition has resulted in formative interventions characterised by process-oriented research, which are radically different from linear interventions characterised by variable-based research (Engeström, 2011; Engeström & Sannino, 2010). Formative interventions differ from linear interventions in at least four ways. The first difference comes from the starting point; while in linear interventions the content and the goals are established before the beginning of the intervention, in formative interventions the practitioners deal with a contradictory and problematic object embedded in their activity, which they inspect and expand by building a new concept. The researcher discovers the content of such novel concept by helping the participants design it. The second difference comes from the process. In linear interventions, the learners are supposed to accept the contents and not to resist the researcher, and possible emerging issues and opposition are considered shortcomings of the design. In formative interventions, the contents and course development are continuously negotiated with the participants who progressively take the lead of the learning process. The third difference stems from the outcomes. In linear interventions, the aim is to fulfil a standardised module that will bring the expected outcomes; such module can be transferred to other environments and still result in the same outcomes. By way of contrast, the aim of formative interventions is twofold: constructing new concepts that may be challenged in other settings to design new appropriate solutions, and building agency among the learners by having them eventually leads the intervention. The fourth difference comes from the researcher's role. While in linear interventions the researcher aims to gain control over the variables and the situation, in formative interventions he or she aims to provoke and sustain an expansive learning process which is guided and owned by the learners.

The Russian genetic modelling experiment, the French Clinic of Activity, the American Fifth Dimension and the Finnish Change Laboratory are all examples of formative interventions (Sannino, 2011). Concerning the history of the Change Laboratory, in the '80s Finnish researchers were starting to look for better ways to improve collective work practice than formative interventions (Virkkunen & Newnham, 2013). The first solution was Developmental Work Research (Engeström, 1996), which was applied to promote large cycles of expansive learning in organisations. These studies, however, tended to last for years, and there was a need for formative interventions that induced medium cycles of expansive learning within few months. The answer was the Change Laboratory, a model of workshop developed from the '90s at the Helsinki University to promote deep and intensive transformations as well as incremental improvement (Engeström, Virkkunen, Helle, Pihlaja & Poikela, 1996). By triggering middle cycles of expansive learning, it helps perform a noteworthy advance in a wider and longer expansive transformation (Virkkunen & Newnham, 2013). The instruments of the Change Laboratory have been designed for theoretical thinking, for designing new systemic structures and for analysing the relationships within and between activities. A Change Laboratory is characterised by three dialectical movements (Engeström et al., 1996), with an interplay between abstraction and concreteness, an interplay between the different voices of participants and an interplay in time between the present, the past and the future. A Change Laboratory typically involves 15–20 practitioners' workshops once a week for a couple of hours for ten workshops plus follow-up workshops. Figure 3.3 represents the structure of the Change Laboratory.

The main tool is a 3 × 3 set of writing surfaces (such as flip charts) to display work activity. The participants sit in front of the flip chart, and a scribe who they elect writes on the surfaces (Engeström et al., 1996). The horizontal dimension of the

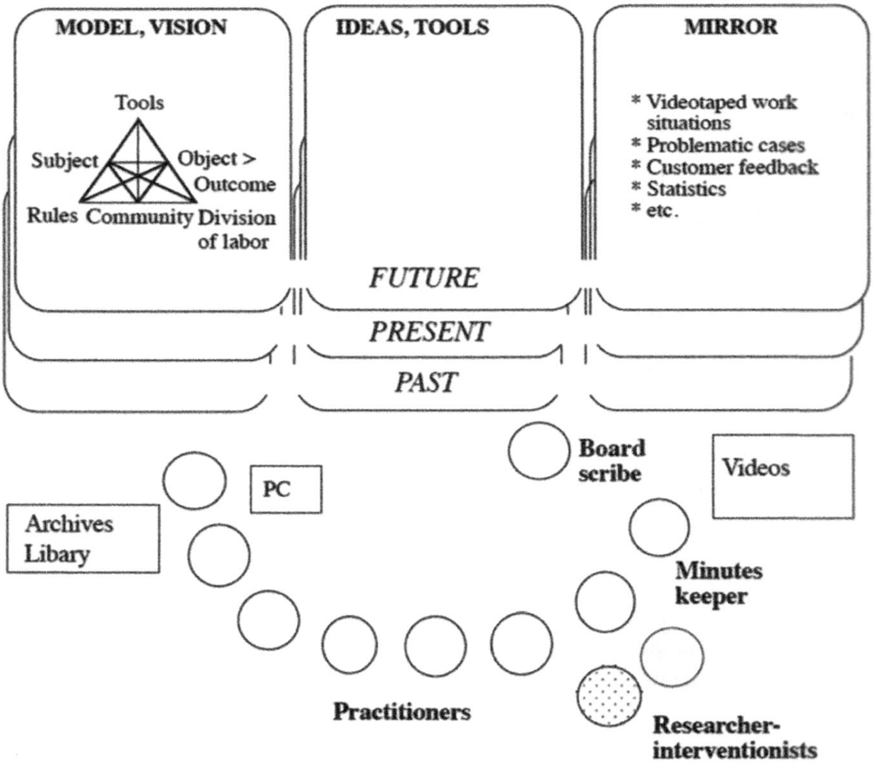

Fig. 3.3 Model of Change Laboratory (Virkkunen & Newnham, 2013, p. 16). Reproduced with permission from Sense Publishers

surfaces accounts for different levels of abstraction and generalisation. These are: model and vision; ideas and tools and mirror.

- At the lower level of abstraction, the mirror surfaces represent the experiences coming from the work practice with specimen or first-hand data. Mirror materials are useful for reflection; they can be problematic situation and disturbances, but also innovative solutions. Concerning their format, they can be videos, documents and figures of the work activity or interviews of customer feedback.
- At the highest level of theoretical generalization, there is a writing surface dedicated to conceptual analysis and theoretical instruments. The triangular model of activity (Engeström, 2015) and the cycle of expansive learning (Engeström, 1999) can be used to study the relationships and systemic quality of the activity system which is being analysed. This helps the participants trace the systemic roots of specific yet recurring disturbances and problems, thus identifying the type of contradiction affecting the activity system.
- In the middle, there is the writing surface for ideas and tools. While the participants move from concrete mirrors to theoretical models and visions, they produce intermediate partial solutions and ideas to be tested. Ideas and tools can be flowcharts schedules, diagrams and layout pictures of organisational structures, classification of interviews, formula to calculate costs, techniques for problem-solving and idea generation.

The vertical dimension of the writing surfaces represents the historical perspective which is important to understand potentials and limitations of an activity system. The three writing surfaces represent the past, the present and the future. Following the different steps of expansive learning illustrated in Fig. 3.2, a Change Laboratory could begin with the participants questioning (1) the present issues; by showing mirrors of the past, the problems could be analysed (2) to trace their roots. Next, the participants could model (3) the present activity and its internal contradiction, which helps concentrate on the main sources of problems. The participants could then conceive (3) a new structure of the future activity that tackles the contradiction with tools and partial solutions. Following, the group could examine (4) the new model to find the concrete following steps to be undertaken. In their daily activities, the participants would then implement (5) the new model and start experimenting with the new practices. These experiments would be video-taped and illustrated during the follow-up workshops as mirror of the future for collective reflection on the process (6) and progressively consolidate (7) the new model and practices.

The step-by-step implementation of the new model would be monitored and planned during the workshops. It is important to note that the new model conceived during this process would objectify the new idea in a way that can be seen and transmitted by all members of the organisation. Such representation could be material or graphic, but also a prototypic case, an observable specimen, or a form of action exemplifying the new principle. Only a part of the outcomes of a Change Laboratory can be observed after the end of the workshops, however, due to the design of this intervention. The Change Laboratory is intended to trigger a middle cycle of expansive learning with the generation of new concepts, while a full implementation in a large-scale cycle would take more time and additional development. Beyond the generation of concepts, a Change Laboratory also improves the understanding of the contradictions of the activity system. Such increased awareness would be valuable for the participants to better deal with the primary, secondary, tertiary and quaternary contradictions that allow the full-scale expansive transformation of the activity system.

The next sections present double stimulation and ascension from the abstract to the concrete, the two basic and complementary principles expansive learning is based on. While double stimulation can be considered the energising principle for collective transformative agency, ascending from the abstract to the concrete is the generating principle for concept formation (Engeström & Sannino, 2016).

3.3 Expansive Learning as Collective Transformative Agency

Traditionally, cognitive theories have defined agency as a consequence of self-efficacy (Virkkunen, 2006). Agency was supposed to depend on the individual's beliefs on his or her ability to exert control over their circumstances. However, such a definition of agency rules out the mediating power those tools have on human behaviour. Sannino (2011) defines double stimulation as "the mechanism with which human beings can intentionally break out of a conflicting situation and change their circumstances or solve difficult problems" (p. 584). While double stimulation has long been considered a mere cognitive technique to improve concept formation and problem-solving, recent research suggests that it is also linked to motives, conflicts and agency (Engeström, Sannino & Virkkunen, 2014). Double stimulation is now considered the basic principle by which will materialises and the key process to investigate the higher psychological functions. It always includes conflictual aspects, in particular a conflict of motives, which constitutes a clash between opposite aspirations or tendencies which occur in situations involving uncertainty. This form of conflict is evident in subjects asking for the courage to make a deliberate choice: an action is volitional only when there are obstacles to carry it out. Together with the problematic situation, a conflict of motives represents the starting point with which individuals intentionally enact their behaviour and influence the world around them (Sannino, 2015).

Double stimulation was first designed by Vygotsky (1978), who in an experimental situation gave a task to a child beyond his actual abilities (the first stimulus) and placed a neutral artefact next to him (the second stimulus). Vygotsky often observed that the child would often draw such neutral artefact into the problematic situation and turn into a meaningful sign to solve the task. In other words, the second stimulus remediated the solution of the problem. An everyday and classic example of double stimulation is tying a knot as a reminder. The event to be recalled is the first stimulus, whereas the knot is the second stimulus, this is the neutral artefact turned into a meaningful sign to solve the problem of reminding. However, double stimulation can be used to manage more complex and conflicting situations. For instance, Vygotsky (1997) referred to the waiting experiment (also named as the meaningless situation) to show the individual's ability to change his or her circumstances (Engeström & Sannino, 2016). This classic experiment has been repeated with variations by Sannino (2015, 2016). A person is invited to take part in an experiment, yet the experiment deals with leaving the individual into the room with no instructions nor tasks. Research has observed the subject's tendency to hesitate until he or she looks at the clock in the room and makes the decision to quit when the hands of the clock move to a position. In such a 'meaningless situation', the wait in the room is the first stimulus; as the time elapses, the wait gives rise to a conflict between possible decisions, whether to leave or remain. The clock becomes the second stimulus, and it is turned into a meaningful sign enhancing the person's will to break from the problematic situation.

The waiting experiment suggests that the individual dominates their behaviour by using external stimuli, the starting point being a conflict of motives. Vygotsky (1997, in Engeström & Sannino, 2016) argued that the only control the individual has over themselves is represented by the power that stimuli exert over their behaviour. By pointing out the initial neutrality of the second stimulus, Vygotsky implied that the outcome of the connection between an artefact and a problematic situation is a creative process of signification (Virkkunen & Newnham, 2013) and that the second stimulus cannot be strictly regulated externally by the researcher. Double stimulation is characterised as a remediation process, since the individual substitutes the previously internalised tool with a new (externalised?) one that is more useful to resolve the conflict of motives. Its phenomenology entails two steps: a design phase of constructing the mediating artefact, followed by an execution phase where the action is performed as if it was automatic (Engeström & Sannino, 2016; Sannino & Laitinen, 2015).

Even though Vygotsky studied double stimulation at the individual level, it should be remembered that for him the higher psychological functions first appear in collaborative action, and only later they are internalised by the individual (Engeström, 2011). In other words, double stimulation can be used by groups and transferred to the Change Laboratory to remediate the aggravated contradictions affecting an activity system. The first stimuli are the mirror materials, the representation of important problems in work practices that the participants are confronted with. As second stimuli, the researcher introduces tools such as the triangular model of activity (Engeström, 2015) and the cycle of expansive learning (Engeström, 1999) to promote a deeper understanding of the intrinsic relationships and the historical development of the activity. Such second stimuli are later combined or replaced with other models and concepts generated by the participants (Engeström, 2011). In other words, the participants use the second stimuli given by the researcher as signs to actively design their own new concept. Both the first and second stimulus typically undergo multiple formulations during the Change Laboratory, which become particularly evident in the construction of the second stimulus, as it involves an ambiguous and incomplete artefact that is progressively filled with meaning and contents.

In the Change Laboratory, the principle of double stimulation is key to build practitioners' will to transform their activity system (Virkkunen, 2006). While the power to bring about change in organisations has been traditionally reserved to the management, during the Change Laboratory, double stimulation causes practitioners to develop collective transformative agency. This behaviour is defined as "breaking away from the given frame of action and take the initiative to transform it" (Virkkunen, 2006, p. 49). Groups express collective transformative agency when they search collaboratively for a new model and new practices. Such agency is transformative because it is triggered by the analysis of the contradictions concerning the activity (Haapasaari, Engeström & Kerosuo, 2014). Rather than concerning here-and-now interactions, it deals with a protracted engagement, a vision and a model to be implemented. Engeström (2011) and Haapasaari et al. (2014) identified six expressions of transformative agency within the Change Laboratory.

1. Resisting the management or the interventionist. This could be expressed as rejection, opposition, questioning.
2. Criticising the existing activity system.
3. Explicating novel potentials or possibilities in the activity. This action could be expressed by speaking of unexploited positive experiences happened in the past or by pointing out that the challenges pertaining to the object could lead to new opportunities.
4. Envisioning new models or pattern of the activity. This form of expression could span from simple suggestions to working on new models of the activity.
5. Committing to concrete change. This resolution is expressed in form of speech acts.
6. Acting to change the activity. The change actions are carried out between the workshops.

Furthermore, transformative agency tends to evolve throughout a Change Laboratory, with a shift from resistance and critiques towards commitment and concrete actions (Haapasaari et al., 2014). Another shift that can be observed throughout the workshops is from individual initiatives to collective forms of agency. Sannino (2010) suggests that the practitioners' personal conflicts of motives are often related to the contradictions of the activity systems they are part of. This means that a conflict of motives often has a systemic basis rather than a personal one. Participants could therefore move beyond resistance by internalising effective second stimuli and exteriorising their internal conflicts.

Relation agency is another concept complementary to a collective transformative agency. A relational agency develops in a process made of two stages that are in a continuous dynamic consisting of (Edwards, 2011):

(1) Cooperating with others to expand the task or the object of activity that is worked on. This is achieved by acknowledging the resources and motives that others carry as they interpret the object of activity.
(2) Regulating one's own replies to the newly enriched interpretations, through the responses that have been made by the others while working on the expanded object.

3.4 Expansive Learning as Concept Formation

The second characterising principle of expansive learning is ascending from the abstract to the concrete, a process which paves the way for collective concept formation. It was Vygotsky (1987) who first conceptualised a two-ways movement between scientific concepts located at the highest level in the development of thinking and everyday concepts placed at the bottom (Sannino, Engeström & Lemos, 2016). While the verbal definition of a scientific concept at the top descends to the concrete as part of an organised system, the everyday concept moves upwards with generalisation and abstraction (Engeström & Sannino, 2016). Again, Vygotsky only considered concepts at the individual level with a 'vertical' dimension, that is from the abstract-concrete dialectic. In doing so, he ruled out the 'horizontal' collective dimension of concept formation, with different individuals having different perspectives (Engeström, 2015).

Engeström, Pasanen, Toiviainen and Haavisto (2006) suggest that concepts represent not only practical tools to master and handle objects, but also visions oriented to the future and ways to create worlds. While the cognitive theories have dealt with concepts as neutral, well-defined and stable entities, Engeström et al. (2006) argued that concepts are characterised by four properties. Firstly, complex concepts are tools and outcomes used by activity systems that evolve historically. Rather than being considered as textual or logical propositions, they should be investigated as embedded in human activity. Second, complex concepts are intrinsically dynamic, debated and polyvalent. Diverse stakeholders tend to generate somewhat conflicting versions, and their formulation involves different perspectives with contestation and confrontation. Third, concepts are oriented to the future; they embed collective intentions, visions, affects, hopes and fears. Fourth, concepts are best learned when they are implemented, reconstructed and challenged in the practitioners' daily activities. For Virkkunen and Newnham (2013), concepts are crystallisations of knowledge and more culturally evolved generalisations. These authors, furthermore, link concepts with the types of variations tested in human practice that are valuable in human activities.

Furthermore, different types of thinking generate different concepts and generalizations. In this regard, expansive learning is characterised by a dialectical view of development with a type of thinking that differs substantially from common thinking (Virkkunen & Newnham, 2013). In everyday thinking, objects have specific qualities and are dealt with as they were isolated and fixed entities, thus ignoring the chain of events which led to their emergence and existence. Everyday thinking also tends to ignore the intrinsic dynamicity and development of objects. In a dialectical view of development, the potential to overcome contradictions plays a fundamental role, and the relationships between phenomena and objects can only be found by studying their historical development and by experimenting on them. Discovering the essential functional relationships of theoretical concepts makes it possible to reveal possibilities that have not yet been accomplished.

It was Davidov (1990, in Engeström & Sannino, 2016) who first studied concepts by distinguishing between empirical and theoretical generalisations. Empirical generalisations are based on everyday thinking, while theoretical generalisations are based on a dialectical view of development (Virkkunen & Newnham, 2013). In empirical generalisations, objects and phenomena are compared to look for identical qualities and parts, and they are categorised according to their external resemblances. By contrast, theoretical generalisations seek to understand how different parts are functionally related and how they complement each other to produce an operating totality, a unit with new properties that belong to none of its parts. Such unit embeds the smallest combination of inner relations and unity of opposites that still preserves the features of the whole. The Change Laboratory makes use of both these complementary types of generalisations. The basic unit of analysis is the activity system, including a theoretical generalisation about its dynamics, inner structure, history and protracted transformation.

Davidov's (1990) principle of ascending from the abstract to the concrete concerns the dialectical process of constructing theoretical generalisations (in Engeström & Sannino, 2016). It is arrived through a collective analysis of how the inner contradictions emerged and how they have been tackled (Virkkunen & Newnham, 2013). A theoretical concept is first conceived as an abstract and basic explanatory relationship named 'germ cell', which is progressively endowed with meaning and details to form a system of concrete manifestations, that is a set of practices. In doing so, the germ cell becomes a fully developed theoretical concept. A Change Laboratory can start the process of generating a 'germ cell' and enrich it with concrete manifestations. The complete process of ascending from a 'germ cell' to a complete and operational theoretical concept, however, would only be achieved within an entire large cycle of expansive learning.

3.5 Preparing a Change Laboratory

A trained researcher is necessary for preparing and conducting a Change Laboratory. There are two aspects to be considered to start with (Virkkunen & Newnham, 2013):

- The involvement of the organisation's representatives to negotiate the aim of the intervention and a mandate for performing it. A project outline is generally agreed on, and this is a first step to identify troubles and challenges that need analysis and novel solutions. The project outline also connects the Change Laboratory with the structure and practices of the organisation and pinpoints the goals and overall structure of the intervention. During this phase of negotiation, the researcher starts to define the activity system with its internal relationships and tries to make hypothesis on the object and the societal need behind it. Some of the areas of investigation concern the major changes that occurred, client dissatisfaction, current initiatives regarding the development of the activity, management's views of the present situation, as well as the units where change has been most pronounced.

- The schedule of the workshops and the data collection on the field. The challenge is planning both the overall agenda and the coming workshop. As part of the second workshop, the researcher analyses the previous workshop and considers the outcomes of the present workshop in planning those that follow.

Second, when selecting the pilot unit for the intervention, the researcher should look for a group that not only has a problem to solve and therefore is committed to change, but is also stable enough to sustain the intervention in the medium term. Moreover, the unit should be chosen so as to possibly represent a prototype to be spread across the organisation at a later stage (Virkkunen & Newnham, 2013). The main criterion to select the participants is their belonging to the organisation (that is the activity system) that will be analysed during the Change Laboratory. For example, in a school, a course or a class can be considered an activity system, therefore the teachers attending the workshops should belong to the same course or class rather than being selected according to the subject they teach. The best number of participants in a Change Laboratory is 15–20 individuals to leave each the possibility to express themselves during the workshops. To be effective, an intervention should also be intensive and uninterrupted; the number of workshop is generally decided before its beginning and varies from five to twelve intensive two-hours workshops on weekly basis. The time between the workshops is necessary for reflection and for carrying out tasks related to the specific expansive learning action being solicited. A period of 4–6 weeks of experimenting with the new practices follows, after which the participants meet for follow-up workshops. Moreover, the effectiveness of the outcomes of the Change Laboratory is significantly improved when they are linked to the management's strategic vision of the activity (Virkkunen & Newnham, 2013). A steering group could help the research guiding the intervention process. While the participants in the Change Laboratory discuss the issues they encounter with no external interference, it is important that the management and the other stakeholders are acquainted with the progress.

Third, the researcher's participant observation is necessary before the beginning of the intervention as well as in between the workshops. Data collection has the aim of helping the researcher to understand the activity system and triggering collective reflection and discussion during the workshops (Virkkunen & Newnham, 2013). Such data is called a 'mirror'. The researcher gathers information to record the customary practices and the emerging phenomena that destabilise the present practices and could lead to their questioning. The key criterion for data gathering is a focus on the relationships rather than on isolated elements of the organisation, including the personal perspectives of the actors. A 'mirror' of clients, for example, could be built by first identifying the composition and the variation of different types, then by choosing most problematic examples or new types. During the workshops, the researcher could discuss the differences between the new and old type of clients and draft a model with the main types of historical change of the object. Other materials that could function as 'mirror' could be the trajectory of cases taken as examples of the new problematic objects and the key actions in the activity. Mirror materials are most effective in triggering discussion when presented as video recorded clips. The suggested methods for data collection are: scheduled interviews with managers, practitioners and clients, observation and videotaping of practices and actions, analysis of documents and practitioners' disturbance diary. The quality of 'mirror' improves when a combination of these methods are used concurrently with one another.

Fourth, during a Change Laboratory, the expansive learning process is divided into actions, and therefore the tasks are planned before the workshops with the aim of promoting specific learning actions (Virkkunen & Newnham, 2013). The challenge is to have the group performing the planned tasks in the limited time available without rushing or hampering the ongoing discussion and problem-solving process. Deviations from the researcher's plan are expression of collective transformative agency, and therefore the researcher promotes and backs them during the workshops with double stimulation. The intention is not to directly target the solution, but rather to turn initial troubles into secondary troubles. Moreover, through a chain of double stimuli, the participants should arrive at the solution of the primary problem with the new model.

The following elements can be considered when designing a task based on double stimulation (Virkkunen & Newnham, 2013):

- A mirror material on the activity to be watched by the participants.
- A question or an assignment based on that 'mirror' is employed to solicit reflection and discussion. This strategy stimulates the construction of the problem namely the first stimulus.
- A method or tool for analysis used as second stimulus to tackle the problem.
- How the learning action is performed, in subgroups, individually or by the entire group.
- The way participants will document the results of the learning action.
- How to discuss, make inference and record the results.

For example, during a Change Laboratory in a school, the researcher could present a video of a lesson (the 'mirror') and ask the teachers to analyse what message about the present practices this tells. Following, the researcher could explain the concepts of disturbance and rupture (see Table 3.1) to help the participants perform the analyses and suggest that they look for ruptures and disturbances in the 'mirror'. This work could be carried out in parallel by the teachers being divided into three subgroups, the outcomes being written on a flip chart and later shared with the entire group. Next, the participants could discuss which of the identified ruptures and disturbances are meaningful, recurring and typical, before writing them on the flipchart for ideas/tools in the present. In this way, defensive attitudes can be overcome with a multi-voiced discussion.

Fifth, the role of the researcher would be to promote collective thinking via an interplay of observations, views and suggestions. The first step is to turn the intellectual motivation to develop the activity into an effective motive, with involvement and interest in taking part in the workshops (Virkkunen, 2006). The participants coming to the first workshop may be already motivated to transform their activity system, but they often see problems from an individual perspective. Consequently, they have diverse ideas on what are the most important issues and how to tackle them. For the researcher, the challenge is to turn these initial troubles and partial motivations into effective motives to bring about change. The effective motive for scrutinising and improving the activity system comes from the acknowledgment that only with a collective action can new opportunities, problems and disturbances be tackled. To do so, the researcher creates an interplay between distanced intellectual analysis and close emotional involvement. While the former—when used in isolation—leads to speculations and hypothetical talk detached from the practitioners' action and motives. In contrast, when the second is used by itself, it leads to moralisation and blaming the individual. This process can be worked towards in four steps (Virkkunen & Newnham, 2013):

(a) Soliciting and clarifying the observations, perspectives and suggestions of the participants ("What do you see in the mirror?", "What do you think about this?", "What do others believe?").
(b) Discussing differences and oppositions between ideas ("What are the differences here?", "Would this be compatible with the idea made by X?", "Where does such idea come from?).
(c) Pointing out that there are two opposite ideas that can be overcome with an expansive solution. Based on the Hegelian dialectical method that connects thesis, antithesis to produce synthesis, the researcher encourages the participants to clarify the contradiction between perspectives and carry on the concrete analysis. The aim is to contrast people's tendency to escape from conflicts, which is generally done by avoiding questioning and moving to abstract conversations.
(d) Asking the participants to look at the opposition more broadly in its context and find means to mediate the contradiction in perspectives. To educate, the participants think with dialectical movements, while the researcher's role is to offer other ideas or viewpoints.

3.6 Designing Tasks to Promote Expansive Learning

This section explains how to plan tasks to promote specific expansive actions (Virkkunen & Newnham, 2013).

1. Questioning. This expansive learning action deals with rejecting and criticising some parts of common plans, practices or wisdom. Rather than distanced rational critique, this expansive learning action entails close emotional involvement. This is done in three steps:

    (a) The trigger is whoever emphasising something that contradicts the current practice, the predominant thinking or common wisdom.
    (b) This brings about discussion and upset among the participants, who could try to restore their internal equilibrium by neutralising the observation with myths or by blaming the individual.

(c) The emotional involvement is transformed by the researcher into a willingness for a detached intellectual analysis. This is achieved by directing the discussion towards the systemic causes of the problematic issues and by underlining the role of tools and other elements of the activity system in causing the negative situation.

The questioning tasks are triggered by mirror materials based on the key and recurrent troubles of the collective activity. This expansive learning action does not generally need second stimuli, and most of the times it is enough to proceed with questions such as "Do you think there is an issue here?", "What do you think it is?", "What makes you say that?". The material should be discussed in depth, and all participants should have the possibility to express their perspective.

2. Analysing. The following expansive learning action is to wonder about the causes and conditions that led to the questioned facets dealt in the previous learning action. The causes are searched for with a twofold analysis: (a) an actual empirical inquiry of the present practice where the trouble is placed in the context of the whole activity; (b) an historical inquiry of the evolution of the object and format of the activity, leading to the recognition of its internal contradictions. The two types of analysis support each other; the actual empirical inquiry gives an overview and hypothesis of the primary contradiction, thus supporting the historical inquiry in the scrutiny of the present situation. The goal is to reduce the diverse troubles at the surface level of actions to a succinct representation of the core causes, that is the main contradiction affecting the activity.

   - Historical analysis. This practice is initiated by a historical mirror of the collective activity. The analysis concerns change events that occurred in the object and in other parts and of the activity system, thus causing a transformation of the activity. In order for this inquiry to be precise and reliable, it is important to collect documents so to avoid relying only on the participants' memories. The meaningful changes which eventuated throughout the history of the activity can be sequenced with the help of a timeline. Following this step, a grid can be used to visualise the changes which took place, so to find qualitatively different periods in the history of the activity. One axis of the grid would represent the timeline of recent activities, while the other axis demonstrates the changes that came about. For this analysis to be based on facts rather than abstractions, it is important that the object and elements of the activity system are detailed with examples coming from the practice.
   - Actual empirical analysis. During the analysis of the present practices, the participants summarise the causes of the disturbances and ruptures they meet in daily activities. They also think of novel solutions and emerging new practices that could lead to an expansive advancement of the collective activity. The goal is to identify as clearly as possible the main contradiction; this can be done in form of diagram, for example, a Cartesian coordinate system with two axes dividing a space in four areas or by using the triangular model of human activity (Engeström, 2015).

3. Modelling. In this expansive learning action, the participants look for a process or an object that contains both sides of the primary contradiction and can thus help evaluate how best to address it. Theoretical concepts, available examples and existing models can be helpful in the search for the new model. Such search tends to generate several competing proposals that should be compared against each other to serve as second stimuli and help model the new solution. The development of a new model requires a reconfiguration of the object and the elements of the activity, as well as their relationships, leading to the emergence of secondary contradictions. The model will be the second stimulus leading the concrete experimentation of the new practice.
4. Examining and testing. This expansive learning action often interacts with the previous one in a continuous improvement of the model and its implementation. In this learning action, the participants carry out thought experiments and focus on how the new model is able to be practically implemented. They try to anticipate matters that could hinder or support change. The researcher encourages the participants to think of contexts that could act as tests for the new model and situations where the difference between the new and the old could be apparent. The practitioners who did yet not participate in the Change Laboratory are involved to support the change effort.
5. Implementing. At this stage, the lead of the expansive learning process has passed from the researcher to the participants. The practical implementation should not be a separate one-time change, but the initial move to overcome the identified main contradiction. Some participants take the responsibility for the implementation and obtain the necessary support from the management. Many practical issues concerning the implementation are dealt with, thus enriching the model, and tertiary contradictions could emerge between the old and the new practices. The researcher videos the planned experiments and presents the videos as mirror material during the follow-up workshops to secure further reflection on the model.
6. Reflecting. This expansive learning action helps the expansive transformation of the activity and its stabilisation. The researcher helps the process by: defining the type of mirror material need, gathering data for reflection, defining the tasks for reflection on the model and preparing the conceptual instruments for reflection. Central issues to be discussed concern the awareness on the key contradictions and how they were overcome, new visible possibilities and problems and actions needed to promote further progress in the activity. Reflection also concerns the circumstances that favoured or impeded expansive learning in the expansive learning actions. At this stage, quaternary contradictions could emerge between the main system and the interconnected activity systems.
7. Consolidating and generalising. This expansive learning action not only concerns the organisational decisions regarding the implementation, the rules and the tools, but also the crystallisation of the new concept and terminology. A document summarising the new model could support this expansive learning action, and by approving this document, the management would pave the way for the implementation of the new model. The document also informs and guides the

practitioners who have not participated in the workshops. Rather than 'freezing' the new practice, consolidation entails a dynamic and sustainable approach, with an endless evolution of the activity while making it the customary way to act. The role of the management is key here to determine that the positive outcomes of a Change Laboratory remain in the local unit, else they vanish. In this regard, when the researcher leaves, a tension arises between the need for continuous development and the inadequacy of means.

In conclusion, this theoretical chapter has shown the main concepts useful for understanding the field research that is presented in the next chapters: activity system, cycle of expansive learning, object, contradictions. Since this study focuses on teachers that want to change their circumstances, a collective transformative agency is important to understand how a sense of initiative and entrepreneurship is developed. The following chapter will tell the Change Laboratory on the field, with a vivid description of the workshops and tasks designed to trigger the expansive learning actions that have been described here.

Bibliography

Daniels, H. (2016). *Vygotsky and pedagogy*. New York, NY: Routledge.

Davidov, V. V. (1990). *Types of generalisation in instruction: Logical and psychological problems in the structuring of school curricula*. Reston, VA: National Council of Teachers of Mathematics.

Edwards, A. (2011). Building common knowledge at the boundaries between professional practices: Relational agency and relational expertise in systems of distributed expertise. *International Journal of Educational Research, 50*(1), 33–39.

Engeström, Y. (1987). *Learning by expanding: An activity theoretic al approach to developmental research*. Helsinki: Orienta-Konsultit.

Engeström, Y. (1990). *Learning, working and imagining. Twelve studies in activity theory*. Helsinki: Orientakonsultit.

Engeström, Y. (1996). Developmental work research as educational research: Looking ten years back and into the zone of proximal development. *Nordisk Pedagogik, 16*(3), 131–143.

Engeström, Y. (1999). Innovative learning in work teams: Analyzing cycles of knowledge creation in practice. In Y. Engeström, R. Miettinen, & R.-L. Punamäki (Eds.), *Perspectives on activity theory*. Cambridge University Press.

Engeström, Y. (2000). Activity theory as a framework for analyzing and redesigning work. *Ergonomics, 43*(7), 960–974.

Engeström, Y. (2009). From learning environments and implementation to activity systems and expansive learning.

Engeström, Y. (2011). From design experiments to formative interventions. *Theory & Psychology, 21*(5), 598–628.

Engeström, Y. (2015). *Learning by expanding*. Cambridge University Press.

Engeström, Y., Pasanen, A., Toiviainen, H., & Haavisto, V. (2006). Expansive learning as collaborative concept formation at work. In K. Yamazumi, Y. Engeström, & H. Daniels (Eds.), *New learning challenges: Going beyond the industrial age system of school and work* (pp. 47–77). Osaka: Kansai University Press.

Engeström, Y., & Sannino, A. (2010). Studies of expansive learning: Foundations, findings and future challenges. *Educational Research Review, 5*(1), 1–24.

Engeström, Y., & Sannino, A. (2016). Expansive learning on the move: Insights from ongoing research/El aprendizaje expansivo en movimiento: aportaciones de la investigación en curso. *Infancia y Aprendizaje, 39*(3), 401–435.
Engeström, Y., Sannino, A., & Virkkunen, J. (2014). On the methodological demands of formative interventions. *Mind, Culture & Activity, 21*(2), 118.
Engeström, Y., Virkkunen, J., Helle, M., Pihlaja, J., & Poikela, R. (1996). The change laboratory as a tool for transforming work. *Lifelong Learning in Europe, 1*(2), 10–17.
Haapasaari, A., Engeström, Y., & Kerosuo, H. (2014). The emergence of learners' transformative agency in a Change Laboratory intervention. *Journal of Education and Work, 29*(2), 232–262.
Leont'ev, A. N. (1981). *Problems of the development of the mind*. Moscow: Progress.
Leont'ev, A. N. (1978). *Activity, consciousness, and personality*. Englewood Cliffs, NJ: Prentice-Hall.
Miettinen, R. (2005). Object of activity and individual motivation. *Mind, Culture, and Activity, 12*(1), 52–69.
Sannino, A. (2010). Teachers' talk of experiencing: Conflict, resistance and agency. *Teaching and Teacher Education, 26*(4), 838–844.
Sannino, A. (2011). Activity theory as an activist and interventionist theory. *Theory & Psychology, 21*(5), 571–597.
Sannino, A. (2015). The principle of double stimulation: A path to volitional action. *Learning, Culture and Social Interaction, 6*, 1–15.
Sannino, A. (2016). Double stimulation in the waiting experiment with collectives: Testing a Vygotskian model of the emergence of volitional action. *Integrative Psychological and Behavioral Science, 50*(1), 142–173.
Sannino, A., Engeström, Y., & Lemos, M. (2016). Formative interventions for expansive learning and transformative agency. *Journal of the Learning Sciences, 25*(4), 599–633.
Sannino, A., & Laitinen, A. (2015). Double stimulation in the waiting experiment: Testing a Vygotskian model of the emergence of volitional action. *Learning, Culture and Social Interaction, 4*, 4–18.
Virkkunen, J. (2006). Dilemmas in building shared transformative agency. *Activités, 3*(3-1).
Virkkunen, J., & Newnham, D. S. (2013). *The Change Laboratory. A tool for collaborative development of work and education*. Rotterdam: Sense Publishers.
Vygotsky, L. S. (1978). *Mind in society: The development of higher psychological processes*. Cambridge: Harvard University Press.
Vygotsky, L. S. (1987). *Thinking and speech. The collected works of LS Vygotsky, vol. 1*. In: New York: Plenum.
Vygotsky, L. S. (1997). The history of development of higher mental functions. Chapter 12: Self control. In A. S. Carton & R. W. Rieber (Eds.), *The collected works of L. S. Vygotsky. Vol 4. The history of development of higher mental functions* (pp. 207–219). New York, NY: Plenum.

Open Access This chapter is licensed under the terms of the Creative Commons Attribution 4.0 International License (http://creativecommons.org/licenses/by/4.0/), which permits use, sharing, adaptation, distribution and reproduction in any medium or format, as long as you give appropriate credit to the original author(s) and the source, provide a link to the Creative Commons license and indicate if changes were made.

The images or other third party material in this chapter are included in the chapter's Creative Commons license, unless indicated otherwise in a credit line to the material. If material is not included in the chapter's Creative Commons license and your intended use is not permitted by statutory regulation or exceeds the permitted use, you will need to obtain permission directly from the copyright holder.

Chapter 4
The Change Laboratory in Practice

Abstract This chapter provides a thick description to make the reader understand the field research, which was carried out in an Italian secondary technical institute. This context was selected for the Change Laboratory, the issue being a dramatic fall in the number of enrolments for a course in surveying over the years. The teaching staff had not fully understood the changes in surveying caused by the crisis in the building sector and the school reform and were still training students to specialise as the pre-reform surveyor, with a curriculum centred on the construction of new buildings. Instead, the school reform and the job market called for a transformation of the curriculum towards the renovation and maintenance of already existing buildings, the environment and territory. The chapter describes the seven Change Laboratory workshops and the three follow-up workshops with the learning actions being triggered, the mirror materials and the topics of discussion. The idea being developed is that in the Grade 5 classes teachers teach around a common interdisciplinary hands-on project entailing the construction of a canteen in a parking lot close to the school. The project is designed around traditional technical topics but is dealt with as it was real, allowing students to make connections between subjects and to understand in depth the core concepts of surveying, and it is coordinated by the workshop assistants.

Keywords Thick description · Change Laboratory · Field research
Double stimulation · Expansive learning · Interdisciplinary project

In Cultural Historical Activity Theory (CHAT), the potential and limitations of an activity system can be better understood against its history. This chapter makes a detailed description of the workshops and field research to make the reader understand the research. The first section makes a historical contextualisation of the field research conducted in a secondary technical school located in Northern Italy. The school reform of 2008 had transformed the school, originally an institute for surveyors, into a technical institute with three courses: surveying, graphics and communication and logistics. After this shift, the course in graphics and communication had consistently boomed with enrolments increasing most in most years, while the course in surveying shrank from four classes in 2008 to only one class in 2015. The section explains how

© The Author(s) 2019

D. Morselli, *The Change Laboratory for Teacher Training in Entrepreneurship Education*, SpringerBriefs in Education,
https://doi.org/10.1007/978-3-030-02571-7_4

I carried out field research in the school and how the course in surveying taken as activity system was selected for the Change Laboratory intervention.

The second section portrays the eight Change Laboratory workshops with the surveying teachers and technical assistants held from February to April 2016. The description seeks to connect practice with theory described in Chap. 3. To do so, it shows the most useful stimuli for triggering specific learning actions and the participants' topics during the discussion and reflection. The following section describes three follow-up workshops held from May 2016 to March 2017, with the development of the idea of an interdisciplinary and hands-on project (in Italian *area di progetto*), and its implementation throughout the school year.

4.1 Historical Contextualisation

This chapter makes a thick description of the workshops and field research to make the reader understand the significance of the context. In qualitative research, thick descriptions portray a research context in writing, and the aim is to thoroughly and accurately describe the relevant contextual circumstances such as the context of the study, participants and connected experiences (Merriam, 2009; Ravitch & Carl, 2015). A thick description allows a sufficient understanding of the context so that the reader can form their own opinions on the research quality and researchers' interpretation. In line with Ravitch and Carl (2015), this chapter will be written in first person to emphasise that this study has been a qualitative research, a unique study conducted in a specific context and historical moment.

According to the CHAT framework, the possibilities and limitations of an activity system can be better analysed by knowing its history (Engeström, 2001). To do so, it is necessary that the researcher engages in extensive field research. This study was conducted from December 2015 to June April 2017, in an Italian technical technological institute in a small city located in the Lombardy region. Previously an institute for building surveyors, since the school reform of 2008 it has three courses: graphics; logistics; CET an acronym for construction, environment and territory (surveying). A fourth course, Geotechnics is part of CET. These upper secondary courses are 5 years long, classifying each year of progression from Grade 1 to Grade 5, and have a final state examination to obtain a diploma, the completion certificate. The major subjects are technical, but there is also a wide range of other subjects that explicitly focus on literacy, numeracy, science, as well as the study of a foreign language (Polesel, 2006). The institute that hosted the research was founded in 1970 as an institute for building surveyors, and since then it has had roughly 500 students with an average of 4 Grade 1 classes. The school reform of 2008 had transformed the school into a technical institute with three courses: surveying, graphics and communication and logistics. Figure 4.1 shows the number of enrolments of Grade 1 surveyors from 2007 to 2016, for 2016 the figure concerns the pre-enrolments (the same figure was used during the Change Laboratory).

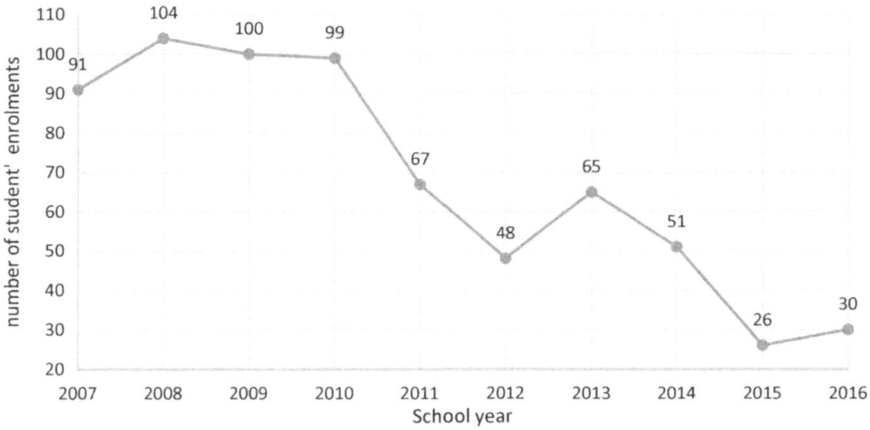

Fig. 4.1 Number of enrolments in surveying from 2007 to 2016

Since a Grade 1 class must have roughly 25 students to be run as part of the curriculum, a drop of enrolments meant that the number of classes of a specific course progressively shrinks up to 1 in 2015. This is not felt as a threat for general education teachers, who are employed in other courses of the school, or more rarely in other upper secondary schools to teach the same subject. By way of contrast, the shrinking of the number of classes for technical teachers is a catastrophe since it leads to their redundancy. If technical teachers want to continue teaching, they have to move to lower secondary schools and teach more general subjects such as math or science. In the context of Italy, however, technical teachers have a private practice and consider themselves professionals rather than teachers. While teaching provides a safety that the private practice cannot give, being forced to teach in general subjects in lower secondary school is considered humiliating by them.

The fall of enrolments in surveying has been observed throughout Italy and has been caused mainly by two phenomena: the crisis of the estate sector since 2007 and the changing role of the surveyor. Architects and engineers have taken over many of the surveyors' functions, to the degree that surveyors can only design small buildings. The fact that a tertiary degree is needed to work as engineer or architect, professions closely related to surveying and which surveying leads to, often makes families opt for general education studies in the lyceum, which is considered more high quality than technical education. Furthermore, the crisis in the estate sector caused a fall in the new buildings constructed where surveyors could be employed. As the teachers will discuss in the fourth workshop, the market transformation imposed by the crisis in the estate sector has called for a new type of self-employed and specialised surveyor who works in close cooperation with other professionals. In line with the European regulations, the Italian School Reform of 2008 was swift to adapt to these changes. Surveying changed into the acronym CET, in English construction, environment and territory. CET implies a diminished importance of building new constructions towards the renovation and maintenance of buildings, while simultaneously placing an increased importance of the competences related to the environment and the territory. In short, surveying has historically evolved with new opportunities for self-employed professionals: estimations, appraisals, certifications.

The reform, however, did not anticipate that both the school curriculum and people's perceptions take time to understand changes to professions. In the school selected for the study, the technical teachers admitted they were still teaching for the old professional. To make an example, construction teachers taught how to design a bridge, but such a blueprint could only be made by a structural engineer. Topography teachers taught how to design a mountainous road, but the city is located in a plain and it would be more useful to teach the students how to design a roundabout. This resulted in a job mismatch for surveyors. Although the teachers already knew what the new professional could do, their curricula had substantially remained the same after the school reform. Writing a programme and preparing new lessons take time, and most of the technical teachers have a second job. Many are also close to retirement, and these are good reasons to continue teaching the old curriculum in the old way.

For the school director, the drop of the enrolments in surveying was a sign of the times with increasing importance attributed to the social media and Internet. From her point of view, the shrinking of classes in surveying was not a problem, as it had been more than compensated by the increase in graphics and communication. The overall number of enrolments in the school had continued to increase steadily year after year up to 6 new Grade 1 classes. This evidence was interpreted by her as confidence that she had done well in her job. Instead, she considered the fact that the surveying teachers had continued to teach the same curriculum as one of the causes that had contributed to the drop of enrolments in their course.

4.1.1 The Field Research

In December 2015, I started conducting field research in the school. My goal was to find important problems that could persuade the teachers to engage in a Change Laboratory. In an interclass council on 11 February 2016, I shared the results of my 2 months' field research with the whole teaching body of Grades 3, 4 and 5 of the school. The presentation focused on two issues. The first problem concerned the students' employment outcomes after school diploma. With the help of a young technical teacher who later took part in the Change Laboratory, I had screened with telephone interviews with all the 132 school students who had taken their high school degree either the previous year or two years before. This approach allowed the graduates before the school reform (18 months after diploma) to be compared with the graduates after the school reform of 2007 (6 months after diploma). In summary, the surveying course appeared to have generated more NEET alumni (not engaged in education, employment or training) after the reform. Furthermore, more graduates seemed to have chosen a different work path than surveying, and less graduates were undertaking practice to enrol in the surveyors' register. My provocative question to the teachers was: "Is it worth to train surveyors if the graduates do not become surveyors?".

The second problem I hypothesised was the unattractiveness of the school open days compared to the competing technical institute, which was located in the same city. School open days are days where families who are deciding which school to apply for their child come over to visit the premises and meet the teachers. To make a comparison, I had visited the school open day of the competing institute. Besides having been built recently and having new classrooms for innovative didactics, the competing technical institute projected a much better image of itself. The families were collected in a conference room, and the school director presented all the courses and the school initiatives, giving the idea that the teaching body acted as a team. Only then were the families shown around, especially the newly built rooms for innovative didactics and the workshops. By way of contrast, the institute hosting this study had been built during the 1930s and had old rooms and furniture. During the school open days, the parents were first gathered in the hall for few minutes, and then they were sent in different rooms representing the courses. The resulting message seemed to communicate competition between the different courses.

After having presented these issues, we initiated a discussion to decide which course would have benefitted most from a formative intervention. The choice was for the surveying course with the goal of increasing the number of enrolments. The participants were 14 teachers and workshop assistants: one humanities teacher, one math teacher, three workshops assistants, nine technical teachers, one of them being also the vice director. Other people occasionally participated in the workshops; these are the school director, the local representative of the industry confederation of the building sector and the local representative of the surveyors' register. The environment chosen for the workshop was the teacher room (with an old furniture, the same as the 1970s) and a classroom that had a smartboard with Internet access to show models and the mirror materials.

4.2 The Change Laboratory Workshops

This section provides a thick description of the seven Change Laboratory workshops. For each workshop, I will mention the learning action I sought to trigger, and how I used the writing surfaces both in the continuum, concreteness abstraction with mirrors, ideas/tools, visions and according to time with past, present, future. I will show the content of the writing surfaces in terms of tables or diagrams and to trace the concept of interdisciplinary project I will report how many times it was used in each meeting.

By comparison with other Change Laboratory interventions, the reader might feel that the workshops run too smoothly. This intervention was, however, carried out within a European project in a formal environment and was supported by the school director. The use of a video recording system contributed to make the participants more cautious about criticising each other, and the process made the participants were aware that they had to work side by side with their colleagues. There were, however, critiques towards the management and disagreement among the teaching staff with expression of resistance. I will quote some of these speaking turns to give a vivid idea of the dialectics going on during the workshops. To show the process of idea generation in vivo, I will also quote some speaking turns where the interdisciplinary project is debated. Another issue is that the participants tended to interrupt each other, so the quotations are sometimes incomplete. All the quotations are translated into English, with substantial changes in the structure and in the wording.

From the methodological point of view, the Change Laboratory and follow-up workshops were video recorded and fully transcribed, and the descriptions here are just a summary of the discussion. The full body of data anonymised (in Italian) is available on *OpenAIRE* (https://zenodo.org/record/838015). For validity purposes (Ravitch & Carl, 2015), the workshops were planned and later discussed with two experts of the Change Laboratory through Skype meetings.

4.2.1 First Workshop, 23 February 2016

The first Change Laboratory workshop had two objectives: familiarising with the conceptual tools and start *questioning the present state of things*. The workshop was joint between surveying and logistics. I first explained them the way the Change Laboratory works and its concepts: cycle of expansive learning, triangular model of human activity (Engeström, 2015). I then showed the participants the figures of the students' enrolments for the school year 2016–2017 *as mirror material of the present*. Table 4.1 represents the first stimulus; I divided the participants into two groups (surveying and logistics), and the task was to find the reasons why we have come to this point.

The two groups had 30 min to perform the task. An idea did not have to be necessarily shared by all the participants to be written on the surface. The following are the reasons of the students' drop in surveying that we put in the 'ideas and tools' of the present:

1. As the overall number of hours concerning technical subjects had decreased, the school reform determined a type of surveyor who is less professionalised.

Table 4.1 Mirror material of the present used during the learning phase of questioning

Course	Enrolments in 2015	Pre-enrolments in 2016
Graphics	More than 60	50
Surveyors	27	30
Logistics	10	14

2. As a consequence of the crisis in the building sector, families enrolled their children to other courses with better employment outcomes.
3. Families may have found other courses more attractive or 'fashionable'; the course in graphics was a competitor of surveying, since both dealt with drawing, and unlike surveying it did not entail complicated metrical computations. For some the fact that the overall number of students in the school has remained steady means that students aimed to enrol in the school due to its reputation, before choosing a course. In CHAT terms, the participants are blaming the course in graphics and communication for the drop in enrolments of prospective surveyors.
4. The lowering of the course goals during successive years which discouraged high achievers from enrolling in surveying.
5. The course in surveying was promoted ineffectively with poor guidance to students for what the course involves, with open days and school tours with little public exposure.
6. The prospective student likely did not perceive the school as providing positive opportunities for their working life. This point is more related to the fact that some students do not care about their school achievement.
7. The technical curricula were not up to date.
8. Some teachers were still anchored to an old view of teaching in the classroom. For example, they were reluctant to cooperate and give up their teaching hours for visits outside the school to learn up-to-date surveying technologies. These visits would have been useful for informing students about industry conditions, but also to promote surveying within the broader community outside the school.
9. Interdisciplinary projects were lacking, which had an impact on the visibility of surveying outside the school.
10. Over the years in Italy, the birth rate has declined, which has led to the overall number of students shrinking.

These ideas are not necessarily compatible one another, yet they represent the different points of view of the participants. Some, such as number 6, are expressed at rather general and are therefore of little use. Others such as the number 5 concern the school and course, and would need more discussion. After having presented the results of the discussion of the two groups, we compared the findings to find shared issues and issues that differ. The common issues were the need for better promotion of the courses outside the school, understanding the conditions graduates would face once they finished their courses, as well as appropriately calibrating the learning outcomes of the courses. While nobody disagreed on the similarities, there was more discussion about the differences and not everybody agreed on the conclusions. However, the participants agreed on the need to update the equipment of the workshops in surveying, and the need for workshops spaces in logistics. The discourse then moved to the need to adopt common rules among the teachers to educate students to behave at school.

During this discussion, the topography teacher openly questioned the present state of things. For her some were shallow in finding the causes of the present state of things:

82	*I wouldn't say that enrolling in other courses is simply a passing trend. I think it's about the students looking for something else. I wouldn't reduce it to blaming regional or industry factors, we can't continue hiding ourselves [...] otherwise we'll not get to any point*

Later she criticised the lack of cooperation between colleagues, since her initiatives are made difficult by the other teachers (bullet 8 above):

146	*We should be more flexible. Yesterday (when I asked my colleagues to bring my class to the University) I was told "I don't know how I can do this". We should consider ourselves very lucky that the University gives us spaces and time. Instead you make such important initiatives more difficult ...*

In another instance, she questioned the choice of the new courses to be activated after the school reform, which was eventually made by the school director against the suggestions of by the committee she had appointed.

221	*As a consequence of the school reform, we had to make a steering committee of technical teachers to find the new courses to be launched in the school ...*
223	*The committee members were discussing which courses were better to match with surveying. After many meetings the members chose the course in agronomy. Of the proposals coming out from this committee, none was eventually considered [by the school director]. Nothing, but logistics and graphics and communication*

4.2.2 Second Workshop, 2 March 2016

The second workshop aimed at making the *historical analysis* of the course of surveying. It started with the summary of the results of the previous meeting. Following this initial stage, in the writing surface representing the ideas/tools of the past, the participants drew a timeline with the important events characterising the history of the school: teaching staff, school directors and courses taught. To retrieve such precise data (the mirror of the past), the participants used an old publication of the 1990s on the surveying course that lay in the teachers' room.

Firstly, the participants wrote their name and year when they started teaching in the school. Five participants had been students in the school in 1970s, and eight started teaching there in the 1980s. Only seven of the teaching staff, mostly workshop assistants, started recently working in the school (since 2013). As second task, the participants wrote in the timeline the various' school directors: five ran the school from 1970 to 1975, while one was in charge for a long period—from 1975 to 2006—followed by a temporary regency of a couple of years, and the present school director has been in the role since 2007.

Third, we plotted school reforms and course changes on the timeline. The course runs since the start of school in 1970 to the school reform of 2008 was the traditional course in surveying. Another course named *Cerere* in agronomy was run between 1984 and 1995, in large part because it was considered the ideal match with surveying. Since 1985–2008, there were two surveying courses: one being the traditional form and the experimental version (called *Sirena*). Since the *Sirena* course had more technical teaching hours than the other, it was more geared to professionalising students. In 2000 another change occurred, the technical institute merged with the lyceum next to it. However, it was the school reform of 2008 which marked the milestone between the old and the new. From 2008 to 2010, working groups were established to find out which of the courses allowed by the school reform could be launched besides surveying. In 2010, the new surveying CET course started with a subcourse in Geotechnics specialising in environmental skills, but this course did not prove popular. The course in graphics and communication also started in 2010, while the year later it a course in logistics was initiated. The school reform has also determined the arrival of two new school professionals: the workshop assistant introduced between 2010 and 2012, and a supplementary teacher for 'students' enhancement' since 2014.

I then invited the participants to distinguish periods in their school history. They found three. The first period was with the school director between 1975 and 2006; the second was the transition between 2006 and 2008; and the third was from 2008 up to present. Interestingly, this period is characterised by both the latest school director and the school reform. The first period lasted almost 30 years and is considered by the participants as the golden era of surveying, which the school capitalised on by having a capable yet controlling school director. The participants wrote on the surface that this period is characterised by organisation, severity, responsibility, valorisation of teachers and authoritarianism. The second period represented a transition between the first and the third period and was characterised by a community of teachers who sought to cooperate. The third period was opposed to the first; it was the period of 'charting a new way' and is characterised by discomfort caused by the reform, divisions, lack of coordination and collegiality.

Figure 4.2 illustrates the historical analysis made with the help of a timeline in the surface of 'ideas and tools' of the past. This banner was entirely written by the participants.

It was clear that the experienced teachers preferred when they were administered by the tyrannical school director who had controlled the school for almost 30 years. A design teacher comments:

This consequence means that, by contrast, the present school director has a defensive attitude towards the students. Moreover, the participants seem to blame her for

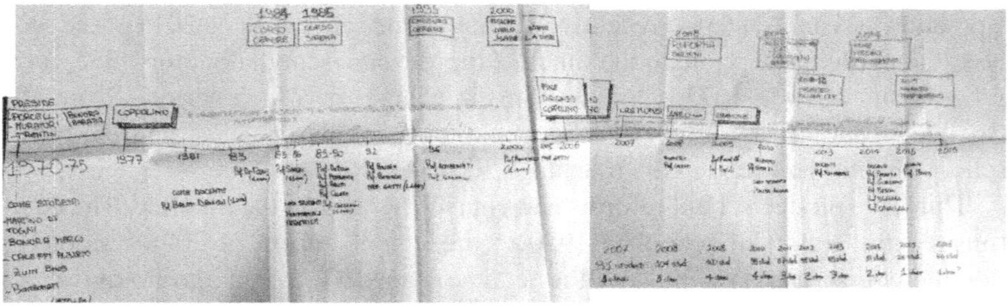

Fig. 4.2 Timeline drawn by the participants during the historical analysis

365	*Notwithstanding that he was a centraliser, he had a protective attitude towards the teachers. If a teacher made a mistake, he would first defend him or her from the parents, and only then tell him or her off privately*

the present state of things. The topography teacher tells me about the previous school director:

540	*He was an engineer (like us). He liked the same things we like, he cared … do you understand?*

The participants also criticise the school reform, another design teacher comments:

605	*I think that the best word to characterise the reform is disorientation. Many of us do not agree with the school reform and think it worsened the previous curriculum. The fact that the new course is not designed to prepare a full technician but rather to continue towards tertiary studies makes many of us upset*

The reform has also caused the lack of cooperation among the teaching staff. Implicitly, the school director is blamed again for not having coordinated the new curricula. The same design teacher contends:

711	*This discomfort has been caused by the reform. We had to understand the reform and each of us was required to autonomously interpret it and apply it in an individualistic way [rather than having a whole-school vision]. Nobody in the school helps us understand the reform and the changes to adjust the programs are carried out individually*

Interestingly, in this meeting, the idea of interdisciplinary project already appeared four times, and it was suggested by the topography teacher as possible solution to overcome teachers' isolating individualism:

731	*There is the issue of time. We have to perform the same things in much less time, therefore we are all rushing. Concerning (the teaching staff's) team work, the interdisciplinary project has always been an interesting activity, but it took time, and we are now rushing so much*

4.2.3 Third Workshop, 8 March 2016

The third workshop aimed at performing the *empirical analysis*. It started with the summary of the previous meeting. To make an empirical analysis based on facts rather than on the participants' memories, we used the curricula of surveying before and the school reform (the mirror of the past and the present). Based on the historical analysis which had identified the school reform as the main difference between the past and the present, the task was to draw a table to compare the surveying course before and after the reform. The participants decided to use colours to emphasise the differences: green for positive changes, black for negative changes and grey for areas that could be potentially positive but need improvement. Such grey areas could be potential areas of development as a springboard for change. Table 4.2 translates the empirical analysis made by the participants in the surface of 'ideas and tools' of the present.

Overall, for the participants the school reform brought more teaching hours connected to general education subjects (literature, second language, ITs) and less hours connected to technical subjects (from 33 to 26 h), but this was partially compensated by the increased duration of a teaching hour (from 50 to 60 min). The unintended result of the analysis was that the strengths led by the reform outweighed the drawbacks. The participants agreed that many changes had been positive for students, the main being: the improvement in teaching hours in literature, English skills and ITs; a new technical subject dealing with the management of the building site; improved didactics leading to a competence-based approach. Moreover, there are potentially positive areas that should be better developed, such as the full exploitation of the professional figures introduced by the school reform (workshop assistants and teachers for enhancement); work experience; the final state examination which should be competence-based. The only real shortcoming was that the subject law disappeared in the new curriculum, which was counterproductive because it prevented future professional surveyors from acting as intermediary between public administrations and private citizens.

In the final part of the workshop, I explained the theory of mini-sized, medium-sized and large expansive learning cycles (Engeström, 2015) to help the participants consider the implementation of the reform as a cycle of expansive learning. When asked to place their course on the larger cycle, the participants said they were *reflecting on and evaluating the process*. Six years after the reform, the participants could reflect on the effect of the reform on the students who had freshly graduated with the new programme. The participants suggested that the following meeting would be employed to hear the voices of the building industry and the local register of surveyors.

Table 4.2 Empirical analysis, comparison on the surveying course before and after the reform

Navigating without map (many containers lacking content)	**Before the reform**	**After the reform**
Subject Law in the triennium	Present	Absent
Subject literature over the 5 years	19 hours	20 hours
Technical Subjects overall in the triennium (without the subject "Management of the building site" below)	33	20
Subject Management of the building site	Absent	6 hours
Workshops and Workshop assistants Co teaching between teacher and ITP	Absent Absent	Present ~~(To be developed)~~ Present, 27 hours ~~(To be developed)~~ ~~(Leasing of laptops for studs)~~ More "forced team work" between ITPs and teachers
Subject English in the triennium	Present in the Sirena Absent in the Traditional	Present in the CAT (plus 1 hour)
IT subject in the biennium	Not present	3 hours in first year
Students' external and internal mobility from the biennium to the triennium	More difficult	Easier
Work experience	Short work experience (2 weeks)	Work-experience (400 hours) ~~(To be developed)~~
Formative approach	Based on disciplines	Based on competences ~~(on going)~~
Teacher for "enhancement"	Absent	Present ~~(To be developed)~~
~~Final exam to obtain high school diploma~~	~~Based on disciplines~~ ~~(**area of project** – interdisciplinary project)~~	~~Based on competences~~ ~~(multidisciplinary simulation)~~
School books Electronical register	paper made absent	Also digital books Present
Duration of 1 teaching hour	50 minutes	60 minutes
Didactics	More (stand-alone) disciplines	More multidisciplinarity
Communication between school and work	Less enhanced	More enhanced
Legend Black: negative Green: positive ~~Grey and crossed out: critical, potentially positive but to be worked out~~		

In this meeting, 'interdisciplinary project' was used seven times to refer to practices that were viewed as good practice. A design teacher, for example, said:

649	*We organised a interdisciplinary project around a common theme. I worked on it, the land valuation teacher worked on it, law (teacher worked on it). It was called "area di progetto"*

4.2.4 *Fourth Workshop, 15 March 2016*

This meeting was a mirror of the present oriented to better understand how the surveying profession had changed after the financial crisis (and consequent fall of the estate sector) as well as the school reform. To do so, the meeting involved the local representative of the *Confindustria* building sector and the president of the register for surveyors. The meeting started with a summary of the previous workshop made by a design teacher to illustrate the two representatives what the group had discussed so far.

The register's president told the staff about modern surveyor's opportunities, such as he/she can potentially open a private practice, thus making an entrepreneurial choice or work as employee. The financial crisis and the school reform, which occurred almost at the same time, represent the landmark between the old and the new: the surveyor is no longer the professional working in the construction of new buildings. There is a wide range of activities he/she can now perform, which constitute mainly maintenance and renovation of existing buildings; role of intermediary between public administrations and private citizens or companies. He/She is a professional with niche specialisation, and this could be accident prevention, energetic certification, or the consolidation of foundation in historical buildings. Such a professional, who most of the times is self-employed, is characterised by their problem-solving and teamwork skills.

The representative of *Confindustria* completed the picture. While the register's president was concrete in their description, the representative of the building sector was quite general, so that the discussion tended to drift away from the actual problems that the participants were tackling. As an employed professional, the surveyor has to be knowledgeable about all types of issues around construction. He/She is a problem-solver, able to spot a problem and to contact the right professional to solve it. School should therefore educate students for working ethics and responsibly when they enter the industry, so as not to be afraid to be highly involved in the building sites or to stay at work until the issues they face are resolved.

However, when the two representatives left a more focused discussion started. A significant observation that one of the participants made was that some students did not have a holistic view of surveying because at school every subject is dealt with as detached from the others. Another reflection point was that work experience should be more qualifying for the students. Additionally, teachers in school should have taught the students how to work productively in groups, since this capacity was at the core of current surveying work. Finally, the teaching staff did not act as an educating community; they send contradictory messages to the students, since they did not agree on common rules such as coming on time to school, handing homework by the deadline, denying permission to leave school before the regular end for petty reasons such as playing soccer. The discussion moved to didactics, and the difficulty of ensuring that students are able to work in groups productively.

The interdisciplinary project was mentioned seven times referring to the past but also to the present. A design teacher suggested that a interdisciplinary project as done many years later in the school could be a solution to move towards a competence approach where students have a holistic understanding of surveying.

227	*I believe that the methodology of the interdisciplinary project that we carried out years ago, and now unfortunately we don't do [this activity] any more, [since it] could be an instrument for the student to have a full-field vision of surveying*

The farm valuation teacher, however, deems it unfeasible:

243	*Since the interdisciplinary project cannot be done, we could try to find few teaching hours to make transversal lessons: starting from a question we move (across subjects). (For instance), we could start from city planning and move to topography, without the need of an interdisciplinary project. It will be difficult but possible. I find it problematic that each time I ask students a question beyond my subject they remain silent*

A few speaking turns later, the design teacher put forward an initial idea of an interdisciplinary project managed by the workshop assistant:

250	*I don't think there is a need for extracurricular time to implement a interdisciplinary project. I [will] explain what I mean: the class council decides to implement a project and makes a plan. Then the workshop assistant coordinates the project and connects with the subject teachers involved*

This idea met resistance by the topography teacher:

268	*Yes, but there are practical problems we have to deal with. For example, we don't have hours where two teachers can teach in the same class. In any case, the subject teacher could carry out a small project with his or her workshop assistant by having the students tackle a practical problem in groups*

Lastly, the vice director pointed out that in the Geotechnics small Grade 4 class he and another teacher helped by the workshop assistant were carrying out a small interdisciplinary project on the transformation of a quarry into a cultivated land. The students were enjoying this project as it was hands-on.

4.2.5 Fifth Workshop, 22 March 2016

This meeting aimed to *model the new solution* to identify the basic contradiction of the course in surveying. The meeting was held close to Easter holidays and conse-

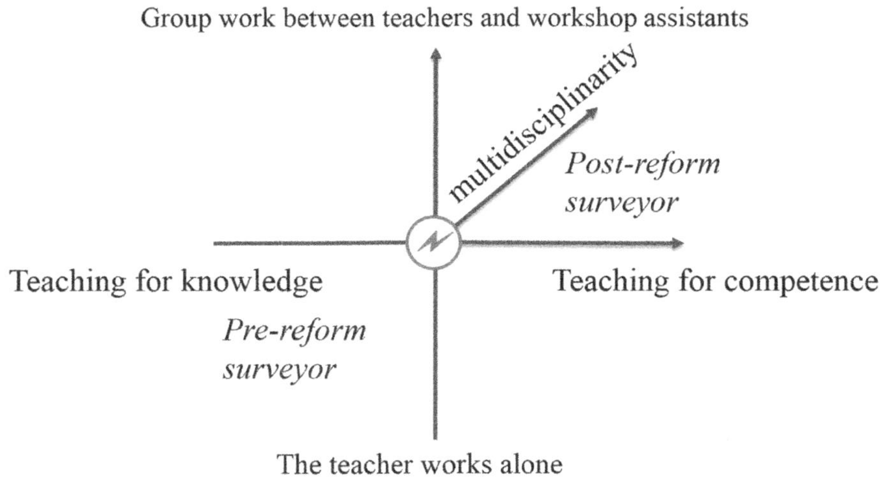

Fig. 4.3 Identification of the main contradiction of the activity system of the surveying course

quently only six participants attended the workshop. I started by making a summary of the previous meeting with the representatives of the industry. According to the participants, this previous workshop did not reveal any information that was new to them about what the surveyor should be like in current industry conditions. In the introduction, I also drafted the main contradiction and I hypothesised as a model explaining the present, as from Fig. 4.3.

The hypothesis I had made was shared through a Cartesian plane. The main contradiction was that the teachers were still teaching for the pre-reform programme, and this clashed with the need to train the new surveyor as called by the reform and the job market. The bottom left area represented the teacher's work before the reform, and the upper right part the teacher's work as it should be after the reform. The horizontal arrow displayed the tension between teaching from disciplines and teaching for competence; the vertical arrow showed the tension between teaching alone and teaching as group—including the workshop assistants. The crossing of teaching for competence and teachers' group work would lead to interdisciplinarity. The red circle with the arrow inside shows the clash between the two fields: teaching for the pre-reform instead of teaching for the post-reform surveyors, which had contributed to decrease the enrolments year after year.

This did not rouse any discussion. The small group where still considering isolated problems and discussed the following topics: (1) students do not have mature social skills, for example, it is hard for them to conduct group work; (2) students' work experience should be connected to specific projects to improve their professionalism; (3) it is difficult to teach surveying when students lack basic notions of how law works, due to this subject having disappeared from the school reform; (4) the common people perceive the surveyor in the old way, and it is difficult to convince them about the new role of surveyor; (5) the external image of the school is negative, and teachers should learn how to market their course better, putting more care in organising the open days; (6) it is difficult to educate students for self-control; (7) the teachers work isolated from one another, and an agreement of co-responsibility would be necessary to work as team and educate as community; (8) the school lacks workshops and equipment.

Towards the end of the meeting, it was clear that the problems had been discussed, and it was time to start thinking of a solution. This was suggested by a design teacher:

520	*I don't believe we can continue discussing on our lacks, from the next time we have to consider concrete proposals or instruments. At this stage I think that we have already performed the analysis*

Given that I had the feeling that the discussion had reached a stalemate, I gave the teachers a task for homework, that is, to think about the future of surveying in their institute. The proposals would be discussed in the following meeting.

In this workshop, the concept of interdisciplinary project was used once by the design teacher:

43	*I think it not enough to make a interdisciplinary project within the technical subjects. A cooperation with the literature it is necessary to create a positive atmosphere and work on relationships*

4.2.6 Sixth Workshop, 5 April 2016

This workshop aimed at *modelling the new solution* and started with the participants sharing the home assignment on the ideas about the future of surveying in their school.

The first proposal came from a humanities teacher. She proposed to start from the students' needs and not from what the teachers know or want to teach. She then stated that teachers should agree on specific cross-curricular competencies (for instance, teamwork) to be developed in the students, and all teachers should modify their programmes to teach such competencies. Students could put together a portfolio to show how they acquired such competence, and this portfolio would be useful once in the world of work.

The second proposal came from a design teacher who made related proposals: organising an interdisciplinary project with the help of the workshop assistants; using workshops to teach student's group work; working by implementing projects in each subject with periodical team meetings; developing a programme on sustainable architecture in the triennium; differentiating work experience; improving the educational climate in the school by establishing and adopting common rules; improving the way the course was designed.

Before the third proposal was presented, the discussion of the interdisciplinary project took over. A first proposal was launched by the topography teacher, the same that in the fourth meeting had opposed it (speaking turn 268):

96	*Let's say 6 teachers, 3 in A and 3 in B. Let's think about Construction, Surveying, and Appraisal of Farmland agree to carry out a common project. The workshops assistants coordinate that project work. We agree on a common project before the beginning of the next school year*

The third proposal came from another design teacher who suggested unrelated proposals: establishing continuity in didactics; that is, the same teacher follows the same students over the years; finding a specific person who liaises with the companies for organising work experience; improving the visibility of the school; activating a course on sustainable architecture in the triennium (this proposal had been already approved in previous years but had been never implemented); choosing only one workshop assistant for each discipline or workshop instead of having each workshop assistant dealing with three different disciplines and corresponding workshops.

The fourth teacher, the vice director, presented a draft paper with the idea of interdisciplinary project:

176	*Here is my project. I propose to resume the old interdisciplinary project I used when I taught the course of Agronomy and that now I teach in Geotechnics. In Agronomy I have much more experience. I propose 3 h per week in the same subject, but we could do it in a different way, for example 2 h of Design and 1 h of Land Valuation. In any case in cooperation with the other teachers and with a workshop assistant as coordinator. The students could present the interdisciplinary project at the state exam instead of the usual pretty long-essay. The topic could be the renovation of a building, but it could be something different, we have to decide this together. In my draft you can see knowledge, competences, contents, and where the various disciplines come into play. Not only technical disciplines but also English, since the technical reports would be written in English. In the case of the subject History of Landscape, the landscape depends on natural shape and on history, therefore the humanity teacher could also be involved). Building to be renewed, 3 h per week, here we should also change our teaching timetable, which won't be easy. Each teacher teaches his/her subject related to the interdisciplinary project, and is coordinated by the workshop assistant. Each teacher evaluates the project according to the subject s/he teaches. This is my proposal, I wrote it in half an hour. We have to proceed with a very concrete proposal, as I see it*

Notably, the last sentence of the vice school director reinforces the method; that is, participants have to come with a concrete proposal. For the topography teacher, who earlier resisted this idea, the interdisciplinary project would be "fully feasible".

177	*To me this would be fully feasible, we just have to plan well when I could come into play with my subject, for example I could appraise the land in October while in November …*

The discussion moves to the role of workshop assistants who is supposed to manage the interdisciplinary project and have the students group work. The workshop assistants, however, felt they could not be the coordinators of this intervention as teachers do not take them into consideration:

221	*We have to start from a simple consideration, I believe that the other workshop assistant would have the same issue. If I ask the design teacher: 'Can we make this interdisciplinary project?', he agrees. Then I ask the topography teacher the same question and he answers: 'Sorry I'm busy this week'. I ask the economy teachers: 'I'm sorry I'm busy'. When I find opposition, I can do anything but giving up. I put my commitment, but if other teachers are against there is nothing I can do*

However, the topography teachers affirmed the concept:

226	*Can you please let me speak? I was proposing a different thing. We (the teachers), who will also be teaching here the next year, propose a project which is given to you (the workshop assistants) to be managed. It won't be you who propose to the teachers "I would like to do this", I will be the one who organises the project*

The fifth proposal is made by another design teacher who suggested reconsidering from scratch the outcomes of the course because the learning outcomes are not in line with the market needs. To do so, a teacher should give up teaching and design the new course in surveying. This proposal was immediately trashed:

331	*I am sorry, but it is useless to talk about the book of dreams, we can only take from our teaching time one or two hours a week*

Eventually, the idea chosen during the workshop is a hands-on interdisciplinary project that builds on the traditional technical topics, allowing students to make connections and to deepen the understanding of surveying. The project should be basic enough to be manageable for students.

Towards the end of the workshop, the school director joined the meeting. The teachers illustrated the idea of the hands-on interdisciplinary project led by the workshops assistants, and the school director agreed it was feasible. She gave two suggestions. The first was to detail the role of the workshop assistant:

331	*Talking about workshop assistant, can I be clear? Many teachers come to me and say that workshop assistants are incompetent, the average one is not useful, I am not talking about you (to the workshop assistant present in the workshop). [...] It is you (the teachers) who must tell them what to do. Two years ago I wrote this point in the agenda of a council, do you remember? You must tell them "please prepare these instruments so that I can perform this experiment or experience" [...] These are things I have told you individually for the first 5 years I was here, and at least 10 times each, then I gave up. You still have time to change*

This speaking, in turn, evidences that there have been long-standing disagreements between these group of teachers and the school director. The second advice was to have the interdisciplinary project approved by the institute council, since this action could allow for changes in the teaching hours. The overall number of times used to mention the interdisciplinary project was 35 times.

4.2.7 Seven Workshop, 5 April 2016

The goal of this workshop was to continue with *modelling the new solution*. In the interdisciplinary project, there were two needs. While some teachers focused on the contents to be taught and how to coordinate the topics within the interdisciplinary project, others were concerned with the didactics that a interdisciplinary project would imply. My proposal as facilitator was to help include active didactics in the interdisciplinary project. To achieve this goal, I proposed a reading group open to anybody, employing the flipped classroom and group work. Volunteers would carry out planned experiments on the active didactics, and in the first follow-up meeting on May 31, the participants would discuss the results. I proposed the flipped classroom because I knew that previous courses on cooperative learning had been organised with no success. In the flipped classroom, students prepare for the lesson by watching videos at home. This appeared good to introduce IT and to free the class from lectures, thus leaving time for active didactics. My proposal was to match the flipped classroom with in-class group work.

Back to the workshop, I introduced a competence approach with its components: knowledge, skills and habits and briefly discussed the SOLO taxonomy and the theory of constructive alignment (Biggs & Tang, 2011) to find the possible learning outcomes for the interdisciplinary project. The starting point was the draft that the vice director had shared the previous workshop. The discussion sought to find the practical arrangements and targeted the workshop assistant' role: although they are often the same, their position was not permanent. A first arrangement had to be made with the school secretary, who would hire them as soon as possible at the beginning of the school year. The other condition was to have one workshop assistant for each Grade 5 class, so that the same person could follow the project across the subjects.

The interdisciplinary project would initially be limited to 99 teaching hours. It would have to deal with surveying in a rigorous way, so that the students could present it at the state examination. The teachers would work on basic concepts rather than enlarging the subject, allowing students to recapitulate, make connections across different topics and subjects and deepen their understanding of the basic surveying concepts. The interdisciplinary project would be hands-on to show in practice what the students already studied in theory, the goal being to develop a holistic view of surveying. Having experts from outside could prove difficult from the organisational point of view. Although based on technical subjects, the interdisciplinary project would also involve general education subjects: humanities with the study of landscape and English with the abstract of the technical report in English.

The group discussed a physical place where to implement the interdisciplinary project, an area that would make the project real. The group found an unresolved area: a parking lot close to their institute. It would be easy to organise school visits, for example to survey the parking lot. The project would have to appear meaningful to the students but also basic to be feasible without pretending. In the following speaking turns, teachers discussed whether to keep it or not:

290	*Even though few years have passed, I remember students finding it difficult to deal with the interdisciplinary project*
291	*Indeed it is difficult, let's come down to earth*
292	*We have to keep it compact*
293	*Good, very good!*

These speaking turns show that the constructive and positive atmosphere during the workshop. Designing a canteen that simply warms up the food prepared in another venue would keep the interdisciplinary project both simple and realistic. Moreover, as the school has no bar or canteen, this topic matches a student's need.

The last issue discussed concerned how to involve the teachers of the course who did not attend the workshops, but who should nevertheless be included in the interdisciplinary project. The other teachers would adjust to the majority's will, who approved of the project. However, while some of them will be happy to participate, it will be difficult to involve others. The interdisciplinary project in two Grade 5 classes could differ according to the teachers who participate. In any case, the first step would be to obtain the approval of the class councils and the department council.

The words ' interdisciplinary project' were used 23 times during the workshop. Appendix A shows the description of the interdisciplinary project as designed by the teachers in an intermediate version dated on May 2016. The model, however, was continuously updated by the participants as it developed, in line with the theory of expansive learning (Engeström, 2011; Virkkunen & Newnham, 2013) discussed in Chap. 3.

4.2.8 Department Council, 10 May 2016

The department council is composed of the group of technical teachers in surveying. While this was not a proper Change Laboratory, the teachers and workshop assistants discussed the implementation of the interdisciplinary project and continued to *examine the new solution*. This meeting represented a turning point: if approved, the project would have to be implemented. Two teachers who had not attended the Change Laboratory were present. This workshop I was present demonstrates that expansive learning progressives outside the Change Laboratory, and once the new idea is generated, it is continuously discussed and developed in the practical implications, with practitioners who had not participated in the Change Laboratory joining the effort (Engeström & Sannino, 2010).

A teacher read the features of the interdisciplinary project, and it was approved. The first query was about the city's regulation plan, whether it would allow for the construction of a canteen. For the students, it is important that the interdisciplinary project would be doable in reality, and the best projects could be presented to the municipality, while simultaneously giving the school more visibility within this broader community.

At this point, the agency was totally transferred to the participants (Sannino, Engeström, & Lahikainen, 2016; Virkkunen & Newnham, 2013). In the following quotations, they claim the ownership of their interdisciplinary project:

222	*(…) The most important thing now is that the Department council approves this idea, which was born during the course (the Change Laboratory), but which is extended to all of you gentlemen*
223	*Indeed, we had had regrets (for not setting up an interdisciplinary project) that we had expressed many times*
224	*Precisely, we do believe in it*

The group continued discussing the timeline of the project and how many hours per subject. Another issue was competence-based assessment for the interdisciplinary project at the state examination. After having discussed such issue with the school director who had called in, the participants concluded it was too early to turn the state examination into competence based with real-world problems to be tackled.

4.3 The Follow-up Workshops

4.3.1 First Follow-up, 31 May 2016

Since the implementation of the interdisciplinary project would start at the beginning of the following school year, and the interdisciplinary project had been already planned; this workshop discussed the innovative didactics that would be useful to implement the interdisciplinary project. After having organised reading group on the flipped classroom and having experimented with new practices, the workshop aimed to *reflect on the new practices*. The volunteers were a construction teacher and a literature teacher who carried out the planned experiments on the flipped classroom with in-class group work. Most of the follow-up was dedicated to watch and discuss these videos as mirror materials of the future. The school director and a representative of the surveyors' register were also present. While in the classes of literature, it had been more difficult to deliver a module with the flipped classroom, the thought experiments in the construction classes had been successful, and students had been enthusiastic.

In design, the flipped classroom allowed for a drop in the number of students who failed the test, from 39 to 12% in a Grade 3 class and from 44 to 17% in a Grade IV class. During the discussion, it was acknowledged that such difference in the success rate was not due to the final mark which also accounted for group work ability. The students acknowledged that watching the video at home and having peer-tutoring in class had risen the understanding of the topic. Based on these observations, the flipped classroom was a promising didactic for the interdisciplinary project, and that didactics to enhance inclusion and success could be used to promote the school outside and attract new enrolments.

4.3.2 Department Council, 14 October 2016

In this meeting, the participants *reflected on the new practice. The implementation of the model* started in September 2016, at the beginning of the school year, with one of the two classes going to survey the selected area. Two technical teachers joined the workshop for the first time, with two newly employed workshop assistants and the responsibility for education at the local surveyors' register.

The interdisciplinary project had started in the two Grade 5 classes. We presented the interdisciplinary project and its aim to the workshop assistants. In the two classes, the project was proceeding in slightly different ways both in the timeline and in the delivery of content. In both classes, the students had to work in groups to share the workload in tasks requiring them to produce documents such as blueprints, layouts, contracts and metrical computations. We discussed the basic methods to have students teamworking productively and fairly. The two new teachers were not convinced about the interdisciplinary project and expressed resistance. One of them, a land valuation teacher, said:

189	*I see many problems in this interdisciplinary project. Firstly, we are professionals coming from different parts of Italy and have different ways to organise our discipline. Secondly, if we look at the time I have to dedicate to this project, I have to take many hours from the regular program. Third, there are always accidents during the year and this project is extremely multifaceted. If I think that I have to wait for data from my colleagues, since all this looks far from simple*

The land valuation teacher raises the tension between the interdisciplinary project and the regular curriculum that will be discussed at length on Chap. 7. The final part of the meeting was spent in budgeting the interdisciplinary project: materials, other professionals, etc.

4.3.3 Second Follow-up, 22 March 2017

This meeting aimed at *reflecting on and evaluating the process.* I shared with the participants the results of the focus groups in the two Grade 5 classes and the interviews with teachers and workshop assistants. Since this follow-up discussed in depth the interdisciplinary project, the next chapter will be entirely dedicated to analyse the features, challenges and potentials of the interdisciplinary project with the words of participants.

From a CHAT point of view, this chapter displayed how the participants are mastering the expansive learning process. It started with the historical conditions that created the need for a formative intervention, and the Change Laboratory on the filed with its multi-voicedness and dialectics. During the workshops, the main contradiction emerged was that the teachers had endured the school reform without understanding it. They had also lost the object of their activity; that is, they did not know what type of surveyor they were training and blamed the others for the situation: the students, their parents, the other courses in the school, the school principal, the ministry of education. Although already carried out at the end of the 1990s, the interdisciplinary project represents a possible germ cell, a practice that is brought back to life with new contents to tackle the issues emerged during the workshops: how to revitalise enrolments, how to work as team, how to improve the teaching methods and embed competence-based approach into the programme, how to improve the image of the surveying course outside the school.

Bibliography

Biggs, J., & Tang, C. (2011). *Teaching for quality learning at university. What the student does*. New York: McGraw-Hill.

Engeström, Y. (2001). Expansive learning at work: Toward an activity theoretical reconceptualisation. *Journal of Education and Work, 14*(1), 133–156.

Engeström, Y. (2011). From design experiments to formative interventions. *Theory & Psychology, 21*(5), 598–628.
Engeström, Y. (2015). *Learning by expanding: Origins, applications, and challenges*. In Learning by expanding: Cambridge University Press.
Engeström, Y., & Sannino, A. (2010). Studies of expansive learning: Foundations, findings and future challenges. *Educational Research Review, 5*(1), 1–24.
Merriam, S. B. (2009). *Qualitative research: A guide to design and implementation*. Somerset, NJ: Jossey-Bass.
Polesel, J. (2006). Reform and reaction: Creating new education and training structures in Italy. *Comparative Education, 42*(4), 549–562.
Ravitch, S. M., & Carl, N. M. (2015). *Qualitative research: Bridging the conceptual, theoretical, and methodological*. Los Angeles: SAGE Publications.
Sannino, A., Engeström, Y., & Lahikainen, J. (2016). The dialectics of authoring expansive learning: Tracing the long tail of a Change Laboratory. *Journal of Workplace Learning, 28*(4), 245–262.
Virkkunen, J., & Newnham, D. S. (2013). *The Change Laboratory. A tool for collaborative development of work and education*. Rotterdam: Sense Publishers.

Open Access This chapter is licensed under the terms of the Creative Commons Attribution 4.0 International License (http://creativecommons.org/licenses/by/4.0/), which permits use, sharing, adaptation, distribution and reproduction in any medium or format, as long as you give appropriate credit to the original author(s) and the source, provide a link to the Creative Commons license and indicate if changes were made.

The images or other third party material in this chapter are included in the chapter's Creative Commons license, unless indicated otherwise in a credit line to the material. If material is not included in the chapter's Creative Commons license and your intended use is not permitted by statutory regulation or exceeds the permitted use, you will need to obtain permission directly from the copyright holder.

Chapter 5
Participants' View on the Interdisciplinary Project

Abstract As Activity Theory is a theory focusing on the object, this chapter concentrates on the idea of hands-on multidisciplinary project that the teaching staff develop during the Change Laboratory workshops. It does so with the words of the people who are involved in the project: teachers, students and workshop assistants. Through interviews to the teaching staff and focus groups with students, the chapter will describe its historical antecedents, the features, the potentials and the challenges of the hands-on interdisciplinary project.

Keywords Interviews · Teaching staff · Interdisciplinary project · Object Qualitative research methods

The first section introduces the methodology in the light of Cultural Historical Activity Theory. The need is to better understand the object, the interdisciplinary project, in the light of what it is and the changes that it entails in the activity system: new division of labour among teachers and between teachers and workshop assistants, new rules and learning tools, as well as new in-class didactics. This section also shows the questions being used and the validation process.

The second section analyses the interdisciplinary project by taking the teachers' perspective. The project features are that it is based on realistic tasks and problems, and it connects diverse technical subject matters and allows students to work in groups. The interdisciplinary project also has diverse transformative potentials: it can change the state exam based on a competence; it calls for an evaluation system beyond knowledge towards competence; it can change the curriculum to make it more up to date; through its advertisement on the school open day, it has the potential to attract enrolments; and through group work, it fights bullying and promotes group work as an important skill set for working life. The interdisciplinary project also faces challenges: it is more multidisciplinary than interdisciplinary; the role of workshop assistants is not fully utilised because of the high turnover and lack of experience; and it could result in an excessive workload for students.

The third section presents the workshop assistants' point of view. Similarly to teachers, the main characteristics of the interdisciplinary project that apply to them are concreteness with real problems, connectedness between subjects and group work.

© The Author(s) 2019

D. Morselli, *The Change Laboratory for Teacher Training in Entrepreneurship Education*, SpringerBriefs in Education,
https://doi.org/10.1007/978-3-030-02571-7_5

The interdisciplinary project has diverse potentials: it will increase employability and be useful for both university and working life; it will facilitate the alignment of curriculum with the new needs of the market; and it will promote inclusion. The shortcomings are that it is interdisciplinary rather than interdisciplinary, and the workshop assistants' role as connecting elements between subjects is undermined.

The fourth and fifth sections present the students' point of view. The Students of the section A only discussed the features of the interdisciplinary project: it promotes group work; it involves various disciplines and is more real, thus giving a holistic understanding of surveying; and it is competence based. The fifth section takes section B students' point of view. The features of the interdisciplinary project are that: it connects the diverse technical subjects, it is based on realistic tasks and problems, and it allows group work. Its main potentials are that it is useful for working life and university, and it has the potential to transform the relationship between teachers and students as a work relationship based on tutoring. It is facing challenges since not all the technical teachers are willing to participate, resulting in an overload for students; it competes with the regular curriculum instead of completing it; and the potential of the workshop assistant is not fully exploited.

5.1 The Methodology

In Cultural Historical Activity Theory, the object plays a key role, as it is the object that provides for the social meaning of the activity (Virkkunen & Newnham, 2013). During the Change Laboratory workshops, the participants developed a new object: a hands-on interdisciplinary project in surveying to be delivered in the two Grade 5 classes. Seen with the help of the triangle of activity (Engeström, 2015), this new object entails new division of labour, tools and roles. A new division of labour among teachers is necessary, because they coordinate their teachings around the common project. Since it is the workshop assistants who manage the project, a new division of labour between teachers and workshop assistants is also called for. The project also entails new rules and tools with in-class active didactics such as group work. This chapter analyses the participants' perspective with interviews and focus groups to better understand the new object and how it calls for a new division of labour, new tools and new rules.

I conducted six individual interviews with the teachers and two with the workshop assistants, while with students I made a focus group in each of the two Grade 5 classes (Section A and B). The following is a list of questions I used during the interviews and focus groups (Table 5.1).

Other themes which I had not thought about when devising the questions emerged spontaneously during the interviews, for example the relationship between the interdisciplinary project and the state exam at the end of Grade 5. The qualitative data analysis was done as follows (Merriam, 2009; Ravitch & Carl, 2015): I transcribed the whole interviews and focus groups and read them recursively to group common themes. The following sections will report a selection of excerpts I translated

Table 5.1 Trace questions for the interviews and focus groups

1. Could you describe the interdisciplinary project?
2. In what ways is the new interdisciplinary project different from the interdisciplinary projects carried out before the reform?
3. What are the differences between this interdisciplinary project compared to a regular project you have participated in?
4. How do you think students/teachers see the interdisciplinary project?
5. How do students/teachers work differently during the interdisciplinary project?
6. What do you think they find difficult in the interdisciplinary project?
7. Do you work differently with your colleagues involved in the interdisciplinary project?
8. How do the workshop assistants work differently during the interdisciplinary project?
9. How do you think the interdisciplinary project will impact on the visibility of surveying?
10. How do you think the interdisciplinary project will impact on new enrolments?

into English. The categories that I use to group the excerpts are the features, potentials and challenges of the interdisciplinary project. Moreover, in the case of the teachers' interview another category is represented by its historical antecedents. The next chapter will tell how these themes were vetted through a participant validation strategy.

5.2 The Interdisciplinary Project in the Eyes of the Teachers

The interviews gather the opinion of two teachers of design, one teacher of topography, two teachers of land valuation, as well as one teacher of agronomy who is also the school's vice director. The vice director is not directly involved in the implementation of the project, but had previous experience with interdisciplinary projects and in-depth pedagogical understanding. He participated in all Change Laboratory workshops, having drafted the idea of the interdisciplinary project. All the following interviewees teach technical subjects, because at that time no teacher of humanities had yet been involved.

The senior teachers already did a interdisciplinary project when it was a mandatory activity carried out during specifically allocated hours before the school reform. However, a new professional figure, the workshop assistant, now helps connect the diverse subjects into a whole, plus the project requires a competence-based approach and students' group work. With these elements, the interdisciplinary project becomes something new from the interdisciplinary project carried out in the end of the 1990s.

5.2.1 What Are the Historical Antecedents?

To better understand the history of the interdisciplinary project, it is necessary to connect it with other projects (interdisciplinary or not) carried out by the most experienced teachers in previous years in the school or in other schools. Firstly, there is a clear relationship between the new interdisciplinary project and the interdisciplinary projects carried out regularly before the school reform in both courses of surveying and agronomy (the agronomy course was held at the institute up until 2000). The vice director, who at the time taught in agronomy, explains the connection between old and new interdisciplinary project:

6	Vice director	*In the workshops we started from my proposal. The idea was to retake the old interdisciplinary project that we carried out years ago when I was here (with the surveyors) and at the course of agronomy. We have retaken a thing we already did*
7	Interviewer	*So what are the differences between the interdisciplinary projects you carried out before the reform and the present one?*
8	Vice director	*At that time, there were 3 weekly hours specifically dedicated to the interdisciplinary project. This year we dedicated the teachers' regular teaching hours to carry out the project in the classroom or in the workshops (continues below)*

For design teacher 2, the main difference is that now there is a new professional involved who connects the various subjects involved.

1	Interviewer	*What is the difference between the new interdisciplinary project and the interdisciplinary project you carried out before the school reform?*
2	Design teacher 2	*In the interdisciplinary project before the reform the workshop assistant, a fundamental professional that we should value well, was missing. Each teacher carried out a small piece of the project and there was a sort of hand-over. The first bit was done by a teacher, the second bit was done by another teacher, and each managed their own piece without understanding the common thread. This time there is a new professional figure that I believe in. If well trained and valued, the workshop assistant could make an overall project—I am not saying between the two classes, but at least in each class. S/he helps the students see the complexity of design, which is the result of diverse contributions. In our society, more and more, design is the result of diverse professionals' synergies, therefore the students should learn how to work in groups*

The new interdisciplinary project can also be traced to a small interdisciplinary project carried out by only two teachers the year before in the same school in the geotechnics course (an articulation of the surveying course).

1	Interviewer	*What is the difference between the new interdisciplinary project and the interdisciplinary project you carried out in Geotechnics?*
2	Vice director	*The project I did last year only concerned two subjects, while the new project concerns diverse subjects. This is the first difference, the second is that while my project concerned a simulated quarry, in the new interdisciplinary project the students go to a real site*

Third, the teacher of land valuation already carried out an interdisciplinary project when he was working in a private school which essentially entailed coteaching.

45	Land valuation teacher	*I don't remember how the interdisciplinary project started many years ago in surveying*
46	Interviewer	*But you said you already carried out an interdisciplinary project …*
47	Land valuation teacher	*When I taught in a private school I did a small project with a teacher of law, I allocated some time to teach together*

Second, the difference between a simple project and the interdisciplinary project is that the students are confronted with diverse subject matters and group work.

40	Interviewer	*Working by project is the first working modality for surveyors*
41	Vice director	*Definitely. The new thing is to carry it out involving as many subjects a possible, and connecting the various disciplines. It is not a new thing, but the effort is to make it interdisciplinary. There are teachers that have the students working in groups, so they develop social competences. The interdisciplinary project is more complex than a regular project and, students develop their social competences even more*

Thinking about the number of subjects involved in the new interdisciplinary project, another difference is that interdisciplinary projects involve disciplines beyond technical subjects.

14	Interviewer	*Did the interdisciplinary project before the reform involve other subjects beyond technical subjects such as literature?*
15	Design teacher 2	*No, it didn't*
16	Interviewer	*Does the new interdisciplinary project involve English?*
17	Design teacher 2	*Yes, and this is the big novelty*

However, the interdisciplinary project carried out before the reform in Agronomy already included diverse subjects, and was presented as a project at the state exam, says the vice director.

27	Interviewer	*Did the old interdisciplinary project in agronomy have many subjects or did it only involve technical subjects?*
28	Vice director	*When I did it in agronomy we involved diverse subjects. We wrote the abstract in English, we had the literature teacher revise the reports, and sometimes statistical aspects for maths. We tried to involve as many subjects as possible. Sometimes we succeeded, some others we didn't. It was not the same old essay that irritates the commission at the state exam, it was a realistic project*

5.2.2 What Are the Features?

Firstly, many interviewees agree that the interdisciplinary project is based on realistic tasks that students could face one day in work activity. For the Design teacher 1, it is closer to the job of a professional surveyor:

15	Interviewer	*What is the difference between the interdisciplinary project and a regular project such as the design of a little townhouse?*
26	Design teacher 1	*I understood it as more complete, and that I started it as if it was a professional job*

The vice director emphasises the fact that in the interdisciplinary project, the students do not have to invent data, but rather deal with real data and problems.

23	Vice director	*At the state exam the candidate refers to a territory s/he knows. In Land Valuation the problem is: "by adopting invented data, the candidate ...", and this is not ideal. Instead, when you go outside and are confronted with concrete data, and not with the data you invented, this is much better*
51	Vice director	*I think for the school it is a big step ahead. It is not new, but instead of dealing with books from page x to page y, you deal with tasks concretely, and there is a good chance that the student will remember*

For the Design teacher 2, the interdisciplinary project is a task that forces students to cope with the problems typical of the working world.

31	Interviewer	*Do you think that this interdisciplinary project is more real than other projects you carried out? I know that the students went on the site to survey, and are designing a canteen that would be useful to the citizens. They also checked if the city planning could allow such a construction*
32	Design teacher 2	*Yes definitely, it is a work that forces the students to cope with the real world*
33	Interviewer	*More than other projects?*
44	Design teacher 2	*Yes, more than other projects because students work on concrete things. They see a map of the area which is not just hypothetical, and this is an absolutely positive aspect*

Although the topography teacher contends that other projects carried out in previous years were to some extent interdisciplinary, this project is different because it is far more similar to problems the students could deal with in their professional practice.

43	Interviewer	*What is the difference between the interdisciplinary project and another project you ran in the school? I know you carried out diverse projects, for example the project on the Shoah last year*
44	Topography teacher	*Do you remember that the last year we carried out the project on the gardens in another school? There is a difference though—the present interdisciplinary project deals with a building requiring more care compared to a garden. Let's say that the students' answer has been a little confused because they are not used to working on concrete things*
45	Interviewer	*So it's a more practical project, more realistic*
46	Topography teacher	*It's certainly practical and realistic. That's what we wanted. This is what we added to what we normally do. As I told you, we have always performed the survey out in the field. However, in previous projects the following step, that is the insertion of this survey into the program of the Real Estate Registry, had only been outlined*
47	Interviewer	*This time they do it for real*
48	Topography teacher	*Yes, this is a problem that we don't normally deal with. Let's say that this time we spent a lot of time on it so that the students could deal with reality. For example, the program does not work if you put a comma instead of a dot to separate the decimals. These obstacles however put the students into troubles and delay their work, so they very much feel the workload*

And this concept is repeated later in the interview:

153	Topography teacher	*It is important that the students understand what they can do and what they cannot do. For example, the site of the interdisciplinary project is close to the railway …*
154	Interviewer	*It is a concrete case study. The students can think about what they know in practice*
155	Topography teacher	*This is what I was telling you before. There are a lot of constraints that you will never deal with if you make a little project of a simple townhouse of 100* m^2

Second, the interdisciplinary project makes a connection between subject matters. For the topography teacher, it will help the students to summarise what they are doing in the different technical subjects, thus allowing a holistic understanding of surveying and construction.

51	Interviewer	*Do you think students sum up what they study in the diverse subjects?*
52	Topography teacher	*As I was telling you before, at the moment they are struggling but at a later stage they will have an insight and everything will fit into place. It is like when you solve a detective story, everything looks confused at the beginning, but in the end everything makes sense. It will still take more time, but in the spring they will arrive to fully understand what they are doing …*

And again:

74	Topography teacher	*However, what we have done so far is not yet connected, every teacher followed their own program, we haven't summarised at all*
75	Interviewer	*I see. Now comes the effort. So far, each teacher has done his or her part. You still have to wrap it up, and this will be the turn around*
76	Topography teacher	*I think so; in a later stage students will understand that they did a complete work instead of examining one little bit at a time. There will be a moment when they will become aware they did a job which is remarkable*

For the vice director, it will help students not to see technical subjects as separated.

8	Vice director	*We retook this thing which is very useful for the students as they connect the various disciplines*
9	Interviewer	*It is based on the idea of competence …*
10	Vice director	*Yes, I see it at least didactically. In doing so students don't see disciplines as detached from each other (continues below)*

Third, the interdisciplinary project calls for group work, a set of social competences important in working life, as told by the vice director in speaking (no. 41) or by Design teacher 2 in speaking (no. 3) above or in the transcript below.

22	Interviewer	*Working by project is the regular working modality for surveyors, so what is the difference between working by projects as opposed to a interdisciplinary project?*
23	Design teacher 2	*I believe that working in groups is important for students to acquire relational competences beyond applying a formula or make a calculation*

For the topography teacher, the interdisciplinary project is an opportunity for group work, as she explains to parents during the school open day:

98	Interviewer	*If I understood it well, the interdisciplinary project will allow students to work in groups*
99	Topography teacher	*We also talked about that with parents, as they asked about bullying in our school. We explained that the class size in the latest triennium is small, since in Grade 3 we have 11 students in one class and 12 in Grade 5. We also talked about group work as an important competence during work, and that through the interdisciplinary project we have them working in groups*

5.2.3 *What Are the Potentials?*

This section deals with the pedagogical renewal brought by the interdisciplinary project. Firstly, it should align well with a competence-based state exam and has therefore the potential to transform the traditional disciplinary oral examination. This is the point of view of the vice director:

10	Vice director	*I do not know if it will affect the state exam, because the critique is that at the oral test there is one question on literature, one on history, the three minute-long question of English, mathematics, constructions … instead, the interview should be interdisciplinary. I don't know if the commission will use the interdisciplinary project for the interview or will just employ the usual round of questions*
11	Interviewer	*We are talking about that in the follow-up workshops*
12	Vice director	*However, the law states clearly that the interview at the state exam must be interdisciplinary, and based on the activities performed during the year or during work experience*

For the Design teacher 2, it will be up to the commission whether or not the interdisciplinary project will be incorporated into the state exam.

43	Interviewer	*Do you think it could be brought as a project or essay at the state exam?*
44	Design teacher 2	*Yes, it could, but remember that the time dedicated to the project or essay during the oral examination is minor. I have a long experience of state exams. If the oral test lasts 30 min, only 10 are dedicated to the project or long essay. We can do everything we want, but if the state exam is not conceived differently, the valorisation of the students' project will rest in the good will of the commission*

Second, the interdisciplinary project can change the evaluation system now based on the assessment of knowledge connected to specific disciplines. For the vice director:

24	Interviewer	*I know this year the interdisciplinary project doesn't concern you as you work as vice director*
25	Vice director	*I will not work on it but I am equally interested because it is a new way to work and a new way to evaluate*
26	Interviewer	*It is a new way but it recalls the old. You already did it*
27	Vice director	*Yes, but it is new because in the last few years we have returned to teaching for knowledge*

Also for the Design teacher 2, the evaluation of the interdisciplinary project will have to include more criteria beyond the reproduction of knowledge.

47	Interviewer	*Also the evaluation should change, did you think about this?*
48	Design teacher 2	*Not specifically, but the experience we made last year on the flipped classroom made me understand that I should think about an array of criteria. I can't just assess a specific knowledge related to my subject, but consider the relationship with the other disciplines and the learning process. The evaluation should therefore concern a specific part of the interdisciplinary project where the student expresses his or her competences in a specific discipline, but also a part, perhaps the majority [of the mark], on the overall performance*

Moreover, the interdisciplinary project can trigger changes in the curriculum, says land valuation teacher 2.

47	Interviewer	*Did you have to change your didactics in the interdisciplinary project?*
48	Land valuation teacher 2	*The only novelty, which pleased me as I had done it during my private practice, is that we surveyed the green area. The students liked this part a lot, I think I opened a new world to them. They normally only focus on constructions, but as surveyors they could also design green areas*

This change in the curriculum is remarkable since during the Change Laboratory, some had criticised the programme as it focuses on constructions and very little on environment, while the green skills are key for the future surveyor.

Fourth, the interdisciplinary project can be shown during open days to promote enrolments in surveying. The topography teacher was the one in charge of the open day and emphasises its features: interdisciplinarity, concreteness.

85	Interviewer	*How did it go in the open day? Did you present the interdisciplinary project?*
86	Topography teacher	*I talked to the parents about our projects. I talked about a project of the gardens we did few years ago. I said that every year we seek to look for something that connects the various disciplines, something practical, etcetera, and I believe they understood the importance of doing so*

In the open day, group work within the interdisciplinary project is emphasised as a possible way to combat bullying and learn a set of skills important in working life.

114	Interviewer	*Hence, in the open day you presented the interdisciplinary project as a useful tool in combatting bullying, since teachers work together and students work in groups*
115	Topography teacher	*The truth is that we do not see any bullying here - at least in the triennium. But the fact the students cooperate is a good way to fight bullying. Furthermore, a course that has a cooperative approach is good because if you work in a private practice one professional has an idea and a colleague has another idea, one person specialises in a thing and another in another thing. However, the need for cooperating is not an invention. Do you remember that during the Change Laboratory we said that an individual work cannot simply be turned into a group work? Instead, in design, many minds have to come together*

5.2.4 What Are the Challenges?

The teachers also identify issues with the interdisciplinary project. The main observation is that as it unfolds, the project is multidisciplinary rather than interdisciplinary. It is true that within this paradigm, the same issue is dealt with in different subjects, but as the teachers do not integrate their work with that of their colleagues, eventually the project is made of small pieces without connection between the topics. For the land valuation teacher 2, the need for interdisciplinarity in surveying had been a main concern during the Change. He explains this clearly in two different speaking turns:

2	land valuation teacher 2	*To me the interdisciplinary project is something interesting but not what I meant. When I asked about the interdisciplinarity during the workshops it was because the students' competences should be transversal and not only sectorial. In the interdisciplinary project I teach subject x, you teach subject y, etcetera. So the student understands that s/he has to study x, y, and z, but finds no relationships between them*
8	land valuation teacher 2	*Land valuation is an interdisciplinary subject. If you don't connect all disciplines, when I ask questions to students I see that my subject is not transferred to the other subjects. A surveyor must have a holistic vision. [...] If we explain our subjects separately we don't give them the possibility of deepening their understanding*

Although the teacher suggests common lessons to overcome multidisciplinarity, the role of workshop assistants should be key, as they could liaise the different technical subjects, thus giving the students an holistic view of the project and of surveying. The second problem is that the workshop assistants are not connecting the diverse technical subjects, the main reasons being their turnover and lack of experience. Concerning turnover, says the land valuation teacher 1:

18	Interviewer	*Talking about coordination, how are you managing with the other teachers?*
19	Land valuation teacher 1	*If I have to be sincere, so far I haven't cooperated with the other teachers or exchanged information. There hasn't been any connecting work from the workshop assistants because they have already changed twice since the beginning of the year. At the end of the year the appointed workshop assistant should return, and I count on her support*

The same concept is repeated by the topography teacher.

31	Interviewer	*So it is a problem the fact that the workshop assistants always change*
32	Topography teacher	*Yes, we said that from the beginning*

Moreover, for other teachers the workshop assistants are not of help in connecting the subjects because they do not have the necessary experience to do so.

29	Interviewer	*You said that a drawback you are observing this year is that the workshop assistant is not the professional that coordinates the interdisciplinary project as we had planned*
30	Design teacher 2	*Don't get me wrong, this is for structural reasons because they have lacked in continuity. Perhaps this is because it's their first experience with this, and they have to build a role which is not yet well defined*

For the land valuation teacher 2, to be useful, the workshop assistant should have a long-standing professional experience.

19	Interviewer	*We thought that the workshop assistant was the figure to connect the subjects. How do you see it?*
20	Land valuation teacher 2	*It is hard for me to understand the function of the workshop assistants. I don't know what they can do, and the only time I worked with a bright workshop assistant, even though I felt uncomfortable, was with xxx. He was older than me*
21	Interviewer	*It seems like you're saying that a workshop assistant with a simple diploma is not prepared enough*
22	Land valuation teacher 2	*It is not a matter of preparation, but xxx has worked in private practice, and knows better than me how to perform a task. If during the lesson I am talking about something, he immediately connects it to practice. My present workshop assistant just keeps silent*

The third issue with the interdisciplinary project is that it causes a heavy workload for students, as pointed out by the topography teacher in speaking (no. 52) above and below:

80	Topography teacher	*At the moment I think that the students see the interdisciplinary project as a heavy job rather than an opportunity. I explained them and the parents that their two Grade 5 classes are good classes, hence we do more than what we normally do because we understand we can expect something more*

The land valuation teacher 2 is one of the most sceptical about the interdisciplinary project; he joined the workshops only in the follow-up. Although he believes that the interdisciplinary project is a burden, it will not be a waste of time.

22	Interviewer	*Do you see an added value in the interdisciplinary project? Or is it just a burden for the students?*
23	Land valuation teacher 2	*Surely a burden. There should also be an added value, I hope to find it at the end of the year. At the moment I find the subjects so compartmentalised and I don't see it. I should check it at the end whether it has been a waste of time, but I don't think so*

5.3 The Interdisciplinary Project in the Eyes of the Workshop Assistants

In this section, I will illustrate the results of the interviews with the workshop assistants. During the Change Laboratory workshops, their role was defined as essential in connecting the technical subject matters around the common project, and at the moment of the interviews, this is the gap to be filled. However, the two workshop assistants interviewed were not working in the institute the previous year and therefore they did not participate in the Change Laboratory workshops. Similarly with the teachers' interview, I will present a selection of the two workshop assistants' interviews according to characteristics, potentials and risks. In one interview, the workshop assistant did not give consent to be recorded, and therefore, I had to write the answers directly on paper. The other interview was regularly recorded and later transcribed for analysis.

5.3.1 What Are the Features?

Firstly, a difference between the interdisciplinary project and projects regularly carried out in the school is that the interdisciplinary project connects the subjects and makes them real.

4	Interviewer	*What is the difference between a regular project and the interdisciplinary project?*
5	Workshop assistant 1	*When I was a student in this school there was no interdisciplinary project. I think it is a good thing both for design and construction, as you put together everything you have studied. For land valuation for example, how do I apply it? You also sum up topography—I remember that when I was studying here we only did a survey once, and it was in the school corridors*

Workshop assistant 2 substantially agrees by explaining in detail how the interdisciplinary project connects subjects through real problems:

7	Interviewer	*You already worked in this school, what is the difference between this interdisciplinary project and the other projects?*
8	Workshop assistant 2	*The students go beyond simple tasks like designing a townhouse. For instance, in topography they are confronted not only with surveying in the field, but also with the procedure for data insertion into the Real Estate Registry. With subjects such as land valuation and geopedology, they deal with the context of public and private green areas, therefore the project becomes interdisciplinary. As their teachers from Grade 3, we observe that students find it hard to connect the technical subjects. For example, during a lesson of Land Valuation, if I ask a question related to another topic, for example if they had the permission to build, they remained silent. It is true that the permission to build pertains to Design, but all the technical subjects are intrinsically connected. This project is good because it will improve their mind-set*

With the interdisciplinary project, the students are forced to get real.

8	Interviewer	*How do you think the students see the interdisciplinary project?*
9	Workshop assistant 1	*I think they would like to be free from regulations and use their innovation. However, the need to be real is part of the project, we pretend that the project will be really built and not be Walt Disney's castle, therefore they must consider the regulations*

Another characteristic of the interdisciplinary project is that although it does reflect the demands of the surveying industry by focussing on group work, the students are not used to cooperation.

11	Workshop assistant 1	*In design they were divided into groups and each had a specific role. To say it better, the general idea of the project was shared while the single tasks were divided between the components. During the evaluation of the students' work, the subject teacher and I figured out that the group work had vacillated, which is natural for young people. If I write the technical report and you draw the blueprint, I can't tell if you are making mistakes*

5.3.2 *What Are the Potentials?*

One of its potentials is that it will increase employability and be useful for both university and working life.

2	Interviewer	*What do you think the interdisciplinary project is?*
3	Workshop assistant 1	*It is the most useful thing, because you put together all you have learnt in previous years in an overall project that recalls all the subjects in a practical fashion. This is very good for working life and even university*

Workshop assistant 2 agrees with their colleague's conception, stating:

1	Interviewer	*How would you define it?*
3	Workshop assistant 2	*An interdisciplinary project, a project that prepares the students for working life*

The interdisciplinary project has the potential to increase the enrolments in the school, provided it deals with an up to date object. In doing so, it has a transformative potential of the curriculum aligning the course with the market needs.

14	Interviewer	*Do you see any contribution from the interdisciplinary project to a possible increase in the number of enrolments?*
15	Workshop assistant 1	*I think that the parents' priority is to choose a school that provides working opportunity for their children, so the interdisciplinary project helps to confront an interconnected real problem. Concerning the increase of enrolments in surveying, although the interdisciplinary project doesn't change the way the school is seen outside, it can be of help for the students' working life. During open days parents ask if surveying can make their children employable, as they observe that no new building is under construction now. We reassure parents by saying that surveyors are still in demand and can be employed in municipalities. Perhaps an interdisciplinary project on restructuring an old building would be more up to date. We should think about something to increase the enrolments, something that is currently happening and which parents hear about on the news*

As it is something practical, the interdisciplinary project can promote inclusion among low achievers.

16	Interviewer	*Do you think that the students work differently compared to regular lessons?*
17	Workshop assistant 1	*I don't know, I see them only during the workshops, but as the project is something practical, even the students who normally struggle are happy to work*

5.3.3 *What Are the Challenges?*

Firstly, the students' workload is not considered excessive for the workshop assistant 1.

6	Interviewer	*Do you think the workload of the students is adequate?*
7	Workshop assistant 1	*At the moment I only see a part of the interdisciplinary project, I don't know what was done before I arrived. I think that the workload in construction and design is adequate, but don't know about what occurred in topography before I arrived*

The following excerpt of workshop assistant 1, likewise 7 above, emphasises the workshop assistants' turnover.

12	Interviewer	*What do you think about the role of workshop assistants in the interdisciplinary project?*
13	Workshop assistant 1	*I don't know what to say. It is the key figure as it is interdisciplinary. It was hard for me as I am newly employed and couldn't follow the project since its beginning*

The same account was given by workshop assistant 2.

1	Interviewer	*How would you describe the interdisciplinary project?*
2	Workshop assistant 2	*It is something very useful for students. However, I was thrown in this situation, the idea was already there when I came*

According to this testimony, Workshop assistants feel subordinated to the subject's teacher. As such, it is up to the teacher to decide what to do in the lesson and designate the workshop assistant's role. This relationship undermines the role of a Workshop assistant to act as a connecting element between subjects.

20	Workshop assistant 1	*The interdisciplinary project is carried out only in certain specific subjects, in other subjects the teacher explains and the workshop assistant remains seated. The teacher has the last word and decides when to proceed with the curriculum*

The same problem is identified by Workshop assistant 2 who proposes to allocate specific time to deal with the interdisciplinary project holistically.

9	Interviewer	*How would you describe the role of workshop assistants in the interdisciplinary project? What problems are you facing?*
10	Workshop assistant 2	*The role of workshop assistants could be key, the problem is that it is not structured well*
11	Interviewer	*It should act as connecting element as you assist each technical subject*
12	Workshop assistant 2	*I am always there in all technical subjects. The problem is that during my hours I cannot deal with the project from a interdisciplinary perspective. If the teaching hour is topography, we only talk about topography; if the teaching hour is design, we only talk about design. I suggest organising the workshop assistant's teaching hours differently. For example, an afternoon dedicated to check the whole interdisciplinary project. We need to allocate a weekly hour specifically for the interdisciplinary project*

This activity would be badly needed as students do not see technical subjects as interdependent.

21	Interviewer	*How do you think the students see this interdisciplinary project?*
24	Workshop assistant 2	*They get involved but cannot understand the importance of this. They don't see the overall project, but only bits. For instance, they know they have the deadline with the Design teacher and only think about design. [In design] they don't wonder about the green areas outside, if the trees can resist the climate, therefore don't ask these questions of the land valuation teacher. They think that the school is like this, and study the subjects as discrete areas*

5.4 The Interdisciplinary Project with the Class a Students' Eyes

This section and the next identify the characteristics of the interdisciplinary projects for the students of Grade 5 A and B classes. The outcomes of the two focus groups are kept separated as the interdisciplinary project was carried out in a slightly different way. Although there are similarities—both analyses point out features of the interdisciplinary project such as group work, real tasks and connection between technical subjects—there are also significant differences. For example, while class A deepens the features of the interdisciplinary project, class B emphasises its future possibilities and challenges. In both classes, the respective Design teacher was present during the focus group, and took part in the conversation with their reflections, with the aim of explaining to students why some choices have been made. I believe it is important to report these reflections in the focus groups so as not to lose the context where they had been made (Ravitch & Carl, 2015). Two teachers participated in the discussion with the students: Design teacher 3 for section A, while Design teacher 1 for section B.

In class A during the analysis, I could only find features of the interdisciplinary project.

Firstly, a student defines the interdisciplinary project as group work.

37	Student	*It is a group work where we work to build and design a public building, in this case a canteen*

The Design teacher 3 explains why group work is particularly important in surveying.

69	Design teacher 3	*[…] Working in groups is important nowadays. As the surveying profession is so articulated, it is hard for a practitioner to have all the competences needed: structure, design, surveying, plants, energy saving. Hence group work seeks to put together all the competences needed to carry out tasks effectively. Group work is not easy and we should learn it; we are not used to it, especially myself. Sometimes I see that only one or two students in the group are working, they all don't work with the same pace […]*

The main concern for teachers is a fair division of labour. Even though the groups are small (only 3 components), some students get involved and may work alone while others could loaf, thus making the evaluation difficult.

80	Design teacher 3	*This creates issues for the evaluation, since it is hard to evaluate the single contributions in the whole project, I can only have a rough idea on who did what and mistakes. However, during group work it is important to understand that what counts eventually is the group, and there is the good or the bad for all*

This testimony below shows how measures have been taken to improve collaboration and thus the quality of the final project. The teacher explains very well how he organised the work and what it means to group work.

106	Design teacher 3	*I believe there has been good group work, since I organised it so that everyone had first to make an individual proposal, thus preparing the best solution. Only after having seen the individual works did I form the groups. Within groups you had to find a synthesis and this must have triggered discussion, I don't think you just drew. The final project you made were all different from the initial projects. It is obvious that you later divided the tasks between the group members, since group work doesn't mean drawing one line each on the same sheet. Group work consists of studying together the problem, only then each group component performs a certain task*

One student finds it hard to cooperate.

70	Student	*I believe that group work has been an issue rather than a help. Because our competencies more or less are the same, in group work it is difficult to coordinate our effort, find common ideas, arrange tasks. If we had worked individually we would have carried out the project better and in less time*

Other students seem not to agree with this statement.

117	Student	*[…] Concerning the organisation, the teacher made recommendations: look at the trees, compare, help each other. We worked together even during the workshops and found the errors of our colleagues. […] It is clear we are not so confident on group work, but …*

Later on, the same student of speaking (no. 70) wants to explain better what he meant:

128	Student	*I wanted to say that if we had presented projects alone we would have lacked details. We put together more minds. For example, I say one thing, and my colleague says "Yes, but we could also add this" I couldn't arrive on my own. Eventually the project has come out better, comparing ideas comes natural, so group work has been a positive thing*

And another student contends:

174	Student	*Speaking for my group, I believe there has always been good dialogue. One component would modify a detail, and immediately send an email to classmates asking them to check it. There has always been sharing both a school and at home by telephone. This is key because we cannot do things alone*

Second, the interdisciplinary project involves various disciplines and is more real, thus giving a holistic understanding of surveying.

47	Student	*It is a work by project*
48	Design teacher 3	*It means that it is a work we perform in a wider area of interest by involving more disciplines*

56	Student	*In doing so, it is more complete, we look at all aspects contemporaneously*
57	Interviewer	*Or one after the other*
58	Student	*Yes, but we take into consideration all aspects*
59	Student	*It is more realistic*
60	Interviewer	*Ah!*
61	Student	*Because in working life this will be the way. If we had to build a self-service, first we would make the survey and see the arboreal species, then present the project to the client. It involves more disciplines*
63	Student	*I think it is useful to understand what we are doing at school, to carry out a project "touching on" all the technical disciplines*

For the Design teacher, the aim of the interdisciplinary project is to also acquire a holistic understanding of surveying.

208	Design teacher 3	*Regardless of the interdisciplinary project, we arrive at Grade 5 with a complex level of understanding of design. But the fact of needing to involve the other disciplines, as you said before, makes you better understand [the whole of the surveying]. For example, if you make a project you must know the area, it is not enough to have a glance on Google maps. You must be aware of the surroundings, the trees, the driveability [...]. [With this interdisciplinary project], we became aware of many things that you deal with when you really work. It is less theoretical and more practical*

Third, the interdisciplinary project promotes competence-based education:

67	Interviewer	*(turning to the teacher) What do you think? Did the students say it right about what the interdisciplinary project is?*
68	Design teacher 3	*I think that the students answered well enough. However, what we want them to understand is that to carry out a project, a vast array of competences are necessary: not only competences given by one discipline but wide competences*

With the words of a student:

206	Student	*Compared to previous years, there has been a leap forward which has been difficult for us. Until last year, we were used to design a little home, or to design a detail without seeing the whole. This year has been much more challenging but also more interesting because we dealt with diverse subjects in reality. We touched with our hands the whole process. Instead, the previous year we carried out the project of a home, but the area was seen on a photo, some topics were not dealt with and eventually it was theoretical*
208	Design teacher 3	*[...] In Grade 5 there is more complete work as you summarise the competencies acquired in diverse subjects, and we deepen the topics we have dealt with in previous years*

5.5 The Interdisciplinary Project with the Class B Students' Eyes

Unlike Class A and similarly to the interviews to teachers and workshop assistants, during the class B focus group's analysis I found the features of the interdisciplinary project, its potentials and challenges.

5.5.1 What Are the Features?

The first characteristic of the interdisciplinary project is that it is a real project connecting the various technical disciplines.

13	Student	*The interdisciplinary project is an activity sufficiently concrete where we connect more disciplines, and for each discipline we carry out a specific function. We regard the overall outcome as positive, even though we would have needed more availability from the teachers, for example for a more accurate survey*
14	Design teacher 1	*Please say your opinions ...*
15	Workshop assistant 2	*What do you think it is the difference between a normal project and the interdisciplinary project?*
16	Student	*We can understand the relationship between disciplines, they are not isolated. For example, in design we understand the relationship between structures and the environment*

22	Student	*Interdisciplinary means that it concerns all the subjects we deal with at school. Let's say that it concerns technical matters hence topography, design, land valuation, management of the building site. It doesn't deal with literature and English*

The students make two examples on concrete tasks they had to cope with.

25	Interviewer	*Is it more concrete than another project?*
26	Everybody	*Definitely!*
27	Interviewer	*How is it more concrete?*
28	Student	*This time we have used a real lot and not an invented area. We should have surveyed the field, and now we are finding issues with the sewage system, landscape and historical binds. In sum, we have bumped into a whole host of problems that we wouldn't have found in an invented lot*
29	Interviewer	*So would you say it's a realistic task?*
30	Student	*Yes*
31	Interviewer	*Can someone make another example of project concreteness?*
32	Workshop assistant 2	*Please speak up!*
33	Student	*For example, we dealt with the public bodies, we had to write the reports according to their criteria. This isn't school stuff but concrete things that one day we could deal with as professionals*

Also for the Design teacher, working on practical problems has a positive impact on the students:

153	Design teacher 1	*I did that and I must say that in my subject it is possible and positive, because students touch with their hands the reality of concrete needs. Indeed they have grown to be able to do more than just dealing with a small house*

Secondly, the interdisciplinary project is characterised by group work, which is a positive experience.

167	Student	*Group work is useful, because there is a lot of work in structuring a metrical computation. One individual alone wouldn't perform it in one month, not even by working night and day*

186	Student	*Group work is essential because we can compare our ides and sometimes we confront each other*

190	Student	*Even confronting with a classmate because he is late, at the end we always arrive at a solution, but we must think it over. If you don't think when you do group work you don't go anywhere, so group work is positive*

5.5.2 What Are the Potentials?

Since the interdisciplinary project entails real problems and is based on projects, it is useful for both university and working life.

34	Interviewer	*Do you think it may be useful for working life or even university?*
35	Student	*For the modality [it is delivered] also the university, because the projects assigned on CAD, subdivisions, etcetera have roughly the same sise [at the university]*
36	Student	*[It is also good for] working life, for example the evaluation of the state of works and the metrical computations. If you want to become surveyor you deal with a lot of them, the interdisciplinary project can therefore serve to understand how to do them*

Group work is also recommended by students since it provides preparation for working life.

182	Interviewer	*What do you think about the fact that 20% of your final mark will come from your ability to do group work?*
183	Student	*Interesting*
184	Interviewer	*Everything starts from the previous year and the flipped classroom, do you remember?*
185	Student	*It makes sense. In working life, apart from the small private practices where you do many things, [group work is necessary] if you work in bigger private practices. As we saw last year, you deal with specific things and always work in groups*

Third, the interdisciplinary project changes the relationship between students and teachers, as it was a work relationship.

296	Student	*I would like to connect with the question you made at the beginning on the differences the way teachers behave compared with Grade 3 and 4. Indeed I have noticed more collaboration. While in Grade 3 and 4 we were given a standardised task: "this is the house and the square metres", here we have more freedom and when we go for revision it's more like a conversation*
297	Researcher	*[Are you saying that] the teacher acts as tutor?*
298	Student	*Exactly! I give him my ideas, and he answers with other types of solutions as if it was a work relationship*

This relationship requires the teacher to mentor the students and provide a formative feedback.

5.5.3 What Are the Challenges?

The first of the issues I detected is that the interdisciplinary project can be hampered by the lack of teachers' participation. Likewise in speaking (no 13 and 28) above, and in the speaking turn below, the students regret it was not possible to survey the field because their topography teacher had not yet started his programme connected with the interdisciplinary project.

20	Student	*We went on the site but left the work unfinished. Topography provides the base for design, and only then we should have started the project by designing the blueprints and more*

In other words, the coordination between Design and Topography has not worked. This outcome is admitted by the Design teacher:

116	Design teacher 1	*There has be the willingness from everyone to get involved in the interdisciplinary project. For example the street project to make a road in the mountains is 30 years' old. Here we live on a plain, therefore it would be better to design an underpass or round about connected to the interdisciplinary project instead of an abstract street project*

Nevertheless:

145	Design teacher 1	*After all we did our job. I believe that at the end of the month we will see nice works. Unfortunately, the project hasn't been shared as much as we had agreed*

Moreover, the same topography teacher joined in two months after the focus group, and finally, the students went for an accurate survey of the lot. Connected to this there is the risk that as the teachers not involved proceed with their programme and projects, the workload for students could increase.

85	Student	*This project is interesting, but as it does not cover all disciplines, the teachers who aren't involved create other things and we end up with a massive workload*

112	Student	*From January, we have to prepare the essays and the project of street topography*
113	Student	*With the subject Management of the Building Site we are running yet another project*

These issues, however, call for better sequencing and coordination between teachers. Another risk is that the interdisciplinary project is considered by teachers as complementary to the regular curriculum. This perspective results in more work being distributed rather than space being given for students to reflect on how they can improve their skills. In other words, instead of considering the interdisciplinary project an ideal corollary, the competence-based interdisciplinary project ends up by competing with the knowledge based curriculum.

86	Student	*We also must consider the teachers' workload because they must complete their programs and simply cannot dedicate sufficient time to both the curriculum and the interdisciplinary project*

In this regard, the students suggest that the interdisciplinary project should be run continuously throughout the school year as a common and main objective:

148	Student	*The initiative is good but should be carried out throughout the whole year. It shouldn't be an additional burden and the program should be simply adapted to it*
149	Interviewer	*That's what we had decided during the Change Laboratory*
150	Student	*It should be something where every teacher works on the same project. For example, last year there was a contest for an important brand making printers, and 6 or 7 students in our school took part in the contest, together with other schools*
151	Workshop assistant 2	*I remember I was there, it was 2 years ago*
152	Student	*We were on Grade 3, and the students from other schools who were there said that they had prepared the project throughout the whole year and had adapted the subjects to that aim*

Talking about connecting disciplines, the students recognise the key role of the workshop assistant but also the challenge of fully exploiting such a role.

101	Interviewer	*Do you think that teachers are working differently in this interdisciplinary project? Perhaps the workshop assistants are working differently?*
102	Student	*The presence of workshop assistants is important to connect design, topography and land valuation. This is because they participate in each subject and have an eye on the whole situation*
103	Interviewer	*Is such coordination functioning?*
104	Workshop assistant 2	*It's not possible unless the workshop assistant is given one teaching hour in the morning or in the afternoon to see the project from a 360 degrees' perspective. We already look at the project but in relationship to design, and we can only see that part. In land valuation the same, while in topography there are bigger problems. The workshop assistant should have their own space, even one hour per week would be enough*
105	Student	*At the beginning, we were told that some mornings would be dedicated to oversee the project on all appropriate subjects, but this never started. It would have been interesting*

When I conducted these interviews, the interdisciplinary project was already running in the two Grade 5 classes. From a CHAT point of view, a potential germ cell, the interdisciplinary project, had been developed into an object and a running activity. This chapter has displayed how the object has been enriched in its practical arrangements, while also positing how it is a multifaceted and contested living entity, which is never established once for all, but it is continuously negotiated by the community (students and teachers mostly) who are working in that activity. The students' perspectives involved in this interdisciplinary project, as well as the teachers and workshop assistants' point of view, with its features, potentials and challenges were summarised with the help of a diagram that is available on Appendix B. The next chapter will show how this diagram was discussed and vetted with the people involved in the interdisciplinary project during a follow-up workshop.

Bibliography

Engeström, Y. (2015). *Learning by expanding*. Cambridge University Press.

Merriam, S. B. (2009). *Qualitative research: A guide to design and implementation*. Somerset, NJ: Jossey-Bass.

Ravitch, S. M., & Carl, N. M. (2015). *Qualitative research: Bridging the conceptual, theoretical, and methodological*. Los Angeles: SAGE Publications.

Virkkunen, J., & Newnham, D. S. (2013). *The Change Laboratory. A tool for collaborative development of work and education*. Rotterdam: Sense Publishers.

Open Access This chapter is licensed under the terms of the Creative Commons Attribution 4.0 International License (http://creativecommons.org/licenses/by/4.0/), which permits use, sharing, adaptation, distribution and reproduction in any medium or format, as long as you give appropriate credit to the original author(s) and the source, provide a link to the Creative Commons license and indicate if changes were made.

The images or other third party material in this chapter are included in the chapter's Creative Commons license, unless indicated otherwise in a credit line to the material. If material is not included in the chapter's Creative Commons license and your intended use is not permitted by statutory regulation or exceeds the permitted use, you will need to obtain permission directly from the copyright holder.

Chapter 6
Reflecting on the Expansive Learning Process

Abstract This chapter focuses on the outcome of the Change Laboratory, a hands-on interdisciplinary project to be carried out in two Grade 5 classes. During a follow-up workshop, the participants discuss the outcomes of the analysis that was described in the previous chapter, and features, potentials and challenges of the interdisciplinary project are discussed with the people involved in the project: teachers, workshop assistants and students' representatives. Since many teachers refer to the interdisciplinary project as competence based, during the follow-up workshop, the participants evaluate the extent to which the interdisciplinary project had been delivered according to a competence approach. From one perspective, this approach is a way to validate research findings: participant validation strategies, also called member checks, are an oriented process centred on the participants to challenge the researcher's interpretations by establishing the conditions for the study participants to talk about the research. These tasks are also designed expected to trigger the expansive learning action of reflecting on, and evaluating, the process to think what else needs to be learnt to improve the interdisciplinary project. The interdisciplinary project will be better implemented during the next school year by solving a tertiary contradiction between the old and the new object, division of labour, rules and tools. This strategy will help train the new figure of surveyor that the school reform and the job market have called for.

Keywords Contradictions · Reflection · Competence · Interdisciplinary project Tensions · Member checks

The first and the second sections tell the results of the third follow-up workshop where the participants were tasked with reflecting on the interdisciplinary project. The first section presents the results of the discussion around the first task, a diagram summarising the findings of the previous chapter on the features, potentials and challenges of the interdisciplinary project. The participants—teachers, workshop assistants and students—agree that the interdisciplinary project is based on group work, authentic tasks, and connecting the technical disciplines, thus moving teaching approach from knowledge based to competence based. There are also issues, however, since the main hindrance for development comes from the workshop assistants whose

© The Author(s) 2019
D. Morselli, *The Change Laboratory for Teacher Training in Entrepreneurship Education*, SpringerBriefs in Education,
https://doi.org/10.1007/978-3-030-02571-7_6

connecting role is underemployed. The second section presents the results of the discussion around the second task on the extent to which the interdisciplinary project has been implemented according to a competence-based approach. The discussion is carried out with the help of a grid with the criteria defining a competence approach. For each criterion, there are specific descriptors spanning from non-competence based to fully competence based. The results of the discussion involving students and the teaching staff make the teachers reflect that they tend to overestimate the extent to which they think they deliver the interdisciplinary project according to a competence-based approach.

The third section compares the implementation of the interdisciplinary project in class A and in class B. In one class, the Design teachers used the interdisciplinary project to teach this subject throughout the school year. Here, the project was made simple enough to be approachable by the students, and the students group worked well, but the teacher did not make use of the formative assessment. In the other class, the teacher taught the interdisciplinary project only for the first semester and the second semester just taught the regular programme. In contrast to the first class, the project was more complicated and the group work did not work well; nonetheless, the Design teacher made use of formative assessment by mentoring the students. The fourth section shows the challenges the interdisciplinary project is faced with, with tensions between the old (disciplinary view) and new (competence-based approach). This tertiary contradiction between the old and the new is visible in the object between the interdisciplinary project and the regular school programme, in the division of labour between teachers and workshop assistants, as well as in the rules and tools for working in groups in the classroom.

6.1 The Interdisciplinary Project with the Member Checks

On March 2017, roughly one year after the end of the Change Laboratory, I arranged the third follow-up workshop to summarise the situation near to the end of the school year, when the interdisciplinary project had been already well developed. This workshop was recorded and later fully transcribed for analysis. The participants were nine teachers, two workshops assistants and four students as representatives of the two Grade 5 classes involved in the interdisciplinary project. Different views between teachers and students were expected to ensure dialectics (Engeström, Virkkunen, Helle, Pihlaja & Poikela, 1996). At the beginning of the workshop, the teachers felt the need to change the organisation of the benches in the room to work in circle. The workshop was organised into two different tasks.

In the first part of the workshop, I presented the diagram (in Appendix B) that summarises the outcomes of the interviews with the teachers and the focus groups described in the previous chapter. The goal was twofold. Firstly, the diagram should act as a mirror material of the present, a task to perform the sixth expansive learning action aimed to reflect on and evaluate the learning process. Secondly, sharing the results of my analysis with the actors was a participant validation strategy (Merriam, 2009; Ravitch & Carl, 2015). In qualitative research, validity (or better, trustworthiness) refers to the ways with which the researcher can claim that the findings are faithful to the experiences of the participants. Trustworthiness seeks to do justice of the complexity of the participants' understanding and to thoroughly contextualise their experience, perspective and life; it is both a goal and a process. Participant validation strategies (or member checks) can use a relational approach to engage the participants to solicit their responses and thoughts on the researchers' concepts and interpretations at various stages during research. The aim of these strategies is to help the researcher inspect and ascertain whether they really understand the participants' responses, and to test their methods of data collection and interpretation.

The participation of the students gave the workshop a special verve as it introduced multi-voicedness (Engeström, 2001). Students are an essential part of the community in a school, and there would be no course without students. Not only could their opinions contradict the researcher's interpretations, but they could also offer fresh perspectives for the teachers to learn from, to produce more developed reflections. It was the teachers who suggested that two students from each Grade 5 class could join the workshops, and the students were happy to come and speak their mind. To take into account the different power relationships between teachers and students (Ravitch & Carl, 2015; Young, 2001), we looked for the most polemic students; although polite, they are generally not afraid to say what they think. At the end of the workshop, they said they had enjoyed the workshop very much.

6.1.1 The Features of the Interdisciplinary Project

This section validates my findings on the characteristics of the interdisciplinary project described in the previous chapter and summarised with the diagram in Appendix B. During the member checks, the participants agreed that the main features of the interdisciplinary project are the following: it is based on realistic tasks, it connects the technical subjects, and it is based on group work.

Concerning the fact that the project connects technical subjects, some teachers argue that humanities topics have also been dealt with, such as the study of landscape and history of buildings. However, these have been tackled only tangentially and by technical teachers, with humanities teachers not being involved. In both classes, the interdisciplinary project has only involved technical subjects, especially Design—the major of the course with 6 weekly hours and partially other subjects such as land valuation and topography. Management of the building site—a minor subject—has been involved only a little bit.

Regarding student's group work, the participants agree that this form of pedagogy has been an important feature of the interdisciplinary project, though necessary only in Design; simulating real design activities dramatically improves the outcomes achieved in the tasks and workload that can be handled by students. However, it seems that in class B, group work did not work well. Class B's students argue that the work that students undertake in groups is different to that which happens in the surveying industry; to be more authentic in the class, it should entail a coordinator responsible for the group. An example can be traced during the planned experiments of the flipped classroom the year before. Second, it was the first year for the Design teacher in class B. As he did not know the students, when he asked how to make the groups, it was decided that the students would form the groups autonomously. This approach was exceptional to the situation, however, since letting students make groups according to their liking has proven detrimental for group work (Johnson & Johnson, 1999).

By way of contrast, the class A's students and the Design teacher contend that group work was more effective. The students had to make a blueprint individually, and only after this first step was completed did the Design teacher make the groups as heterogeneous as possible according to the blueprints. In groups of three individuals, they had to discuss their blueprints they had created separately and come out with a new design that synthesised elements from all three of their drafts.

In any case, for both Design teachers, the main concern on group work was to avoid students' loafing, that is some members in the group carried out most of the work, while others were not doing anything. This misconduct is perceived by teachers as a matter of fairness; it is unfair to give a good mark to a student who did make a significant contribution. However, I subsequently learnt from teachers and students that in both classes, group work had not worked well, and diverse students had loafed.

Another feature of the interdisciplinary project acknowledged by the whole group during the member checks is that it promotes a competence-based approach and a holistic understanding of surveying. The class A's Design teacher carried out the interdisciplinary project throughout the whole school year, and when possible used it as 'an excuse' to embed the other topics of the programme he wanted to teach, indicating that he taught according to a competence-based approach.

6.1.2 The Potentials of the Interdisciplinary Project

This section deals with the validation of my findings on the potentials of the interdisciplinary project. The participants agree that if presented during the open days, the interdisciplinary project can promote enrolments in surveying. This is done by explaining the parents that in surveying students tackle a need felt as important by the city habitants with a concrete project in a known area of the city. The teachers agree that the interdisciplinary project can also contribute to make the course more up to date. For example, it was the first time that the students dealt with the transformation of gardens related to an historical building. This helps the course in surveying moving from the issues related to constructions towards environment and territory, thus making the future professional more in line with the demands of the industry. The teachers comment that this potential has also been used to promote the course in surveying during the open days.

My finding that the interdisciplinary project can make the state exam more competence based did not raise any discussion or agreement. This result is because no student had decided so far to present their project at the state exam. The participants agree that the interdisciplinary project can, however, make the students more employable. This potential is true in principle, with students more capable of dealing with issues they could face one day at work such as the sewage system and plants of buildings, but it is also true in practice, with the students being able to present a portfolio at their job interviews containing their work.

The students agree only to a limited extent that, as it is based on concrete tasks, the interdisciplinary project has brought inclusion among some 'hands-on' learners. This triggers a discussion on an alleged students' scholastic attitude to be overcome in class B. While the workshop assistant of class B would have expected more proactivity, autonomy and problem-solving attitude in carrying out the interdisciplinary project, the students do not understand what it means to have a scholastic attitude, given the fact they are students and not professionals. Moreover, the class B's students and a Design teacher suggest that the project may indeed have been too difficult, thus hampering their proactiveness and autonomy in carrying out the interdisciplinary project. For the class B's Design teacher, the interdisciplinary project was carried out throughout the whole year, and disciplinary aspects of design were discarded to give students time to learn according to a competence-based approach.

6.1.3 The Challenges of the Interdisciplinary Project

This section deals with the validation of my findings regarding the challenges faced by the interdisciplinary project. Most of the interviews and focus groups showed that harnessing the workshop assistants' potential is the most important challenge. There have been three orders of problems: a) in class A, there has been a turnover of three workshop assistants over the school year, the first being appointed one month after the beginning of school, that year; b) in both classes, no time has been allocated for workshop assistants to take the lead with lessons aimed at connecting the technical subjects; c) most teachers have the feeling that the workshop assistants do not have enough expertise to assert a leading role. However, from the class A's topography teacher point of view, the workshop assistants' turnover has not hindered her work, and while the position was still vacant, the other class' workshop assistant came to help students perform the field survey.

Both teachers and workshop assistants agree that planning should be necessary to help the workshop assistant have a leading role, yet the main dispute relates to who should write such plan—whether the teachers or the workshop assistants. The teachers argue that workshop assistant should propose the plan and the workshop assistants argue the opposite. This disagreement is because workshop assistants could write the plan, but the teachers are the only responsible for the course contents. The final compromise that was made in the workshop itself was to discuss the division of labour in the next follow-up workshop or at the beginning of the school year.

Another issue is that the project has been more multidisciplinary than interdisciplinary. In both classes, only sometimes the students had seen the interdisciplinary project from a holistic perspective, but most of the times they only considered the interdisciplinary project from the point of view of the specific disciplines. This disparity is because the workshop assistant has played a minor role. The proposal is to allocate specific hours for interdisciplinarity, and this would reduce the risk that the workload for students becomes too heavy.

6.2 Is the Interdisciplinary Project Implemented According to a Competence-Based Approach?

The second part of the follow-up workshop aimed at the action of reflecting on and evaluating the expansive learning process to find what else needs to be learnt (Engeström & Sannino, 2010). During the interviews and focus groups described in the previous chapter, most of the teachers referred to the interdisciplinary approach as competence based. I then organised a discussion workshop between the participants to explore how they thought the interdisciplinary project fit within this competence-based framework, with the intention of also addressing the issue of how to improve the project. To achieve these goals, I used evaluation grids, and for each criterion, the participants rated the extent to which the interdisciplinary project was delivered according to a competence-based approach. The assessment grid (or rubric) was taken from Sturing, Biemans, Mulder and De Bruijn (2011) and from Koenen, Dochy and Berghmans (2015), and translated into Italian. The grid used as mirror material of the present was composed of 12 rows with the criteria, and 5 columns indicating the levels of competence: (1) not competence based; (2) starting to be competence based; (3) only partially competence based; (4) largely competence based; (5) completely competence based. The rubric was a new instrument for the teaching staff who had never undertaken pedagogical training to develop a focus based on competencies. The participants first discussed the grid in couple to become familiar with the format. Marton (2014) suggests that to learn, individuals need to discern between at least two meanings against a background of invariance; the grid aimed at having the participants reflect criterion after criterion on the differences between a knowledge-based approach and a competence-based approach. The following bullet points report the outcomes of the discussion for each of the 12 criteria and the ranking attributed by teachers and students:

(1) *The study programme is based on founding tasks, work processes and competences (the qualification profile).* Here, I explained the term learning outcomes as it should be in competence-based approaches. It is unclear to what extent the teachers use the qualification profile for their course programme; they tend to rely more on the content given by the Ministry of Education. The impact of this approach is that the course curricula are far from being written in.

(2) *Teachers put at the centre complex and founding vocational problems.* Here, I explained to the teachers the meaning of this criterion; the interdisciplinary project does put at the centre an important and valuable vocational problem to be resolved holistically by the students. This criterion can therefore be considered as fulfilled.
(3) *The learning activities take place in diverse, significant and concrete professional situations.* For the students, the interdisciplinary project ranks on level 3, which means it is viewed as only partially competence based. The descriptor for level 3 is "Inside and outside school, the learning activities partially take place in concrete and meaningful contexts. From time to time teachers connect in-class experience and practical experience". By way of contrast, the teachers consider the interdisciplinary project on level 4, which means largely competence based; the descriptor for this level is "Inside and outside school, the students often work individually or in team on learning activities taking place in several contexts of concrete and meaningful practice. A connection is often made between in-class learning and learning through practical experience".
(4) *Knowledge, skills and attitudes are integrated.* For the students the interdisciplinary project ranks on level 3, only partially competence based, the descriptor is "Knowledge, skills and attitudes are integrated into some parts of the programme, but the three aspects are assessed separately". In other words, the students have the feeling that knowledge, skills and attitudes are still taught as separate elements from each other, in their curriculum.
(5) *The students are regularly evaluated.* For the students the interdisciplinary project ranks on level 2, that is starting to be competence based, the descriptor for that level is "the assessment takes place several times during the learning process, and it is qualifying. Students seldom assess the development of their competence. Professional practice is rarely involved in the assessment". There is a clear lack of self-assessment practices, with assessment mostly relating to topics based on acquiring knowledge.
(6) *The students are encouraged to reflect on their learning process.* Here the teachers ranked the interdisciplinary project on level 4, namely largely competence based. The descriptor for this is "Students are often encouraged to reflect on their learning and on learning outcomes". Teachers argued that students are often encouraged to reflect on their mistakes after summative assessment. Students are not assessed, however, for the quality of their reflections. This omission shows that summative assessment does not guide learning and so does not promote reflection (Biggs & Tang, 2011).
(7) *The study programme is organised in such a way that students progressively lead their own learning.* For the students the interdisciplinary project can be ranked between 2 (starting to be competence based) and 3 (partially competence based). The descriptors for 2 are: "There are rare possibilities for students to self-guide their learning", while for 3 "There are some possibilities for stu-

dents to self-guide their learning. Students have some influence on their own learning process. Both the student and the teacher are co-responsible for the student's learning process".

(8) *The study programme is flexible.* All the students rank the course flexibility at level 1 that is not competence based. The descriptor is "The study programme is the same for each learner. There is no possibility to change it for specific students". For the teachers the level is 2, "starting to be competence based, with the descriptor "The study programme is the same for each student, but there is the possibility to follow it at own pace". During the workshop, the teachers argued that there are students who are allowed to hand their homework later. The students' reply to this claim was that this accommodation is not an example of course flexibility, since in the end each student is expected to produce the same outcome.

(9) *The teacher's directions are personalised to the specific student's learning needs.* The couple of students of class B rank this criterion on level 3, which means only partially competence based, the descriptor being "The teacher is a coach and an expert. The teacher offers directions that are partially adapted to the student's learning needs". They probably refer to their Design teacher and the periodical project revisions. The other couple of students argued that it depends very much on the teacher and preferred not to express their opinion in their evaluation.

(10) *The study programme also considers competences related to citizenship, career and learning.* Most of the participants do not know what is meant by educating for citizenship. These competences were explained to the whole group by the teacher of literature. It is unlikely that such key competences are taken into consideration and embedded into the respective curricula.

(11) *Role of assessment.* Here I explained to teachers and students what formative and summative assessment mean (described in Chap. 2). Unfortunately, formative assessment is a practice that teachers do not know much about. In class A, only the literature teacher made use of feedback that she gathers from formative tasks. Within the interdisciplinary project, in class B the Design teacher made group revisions of the state of the project, and this peer mentoring constituted a form of formative assessment.

(12) *Plurality of sources of information for assessment.* I explained the meaning of this criterion to the teachers. It appeared that teachers at this stage only use their point of view to assess the performance of students as well as the effectiveness of their tasks.

Hence, during the discussion it emerged that the teachers took for granted that teaching using a interdisciplinary project makes the curriculum competence-based, while students see possible improvements in the way theinterdisciplinary project should be delivered. This technique could entail: improved use of formative assessment; personalisation of the programme according to the students' needs; integration of assessment with forms of self-assessment and reflection; better connection of the school activities with outer school activities and improved integration of knowledge, skills and attitudes.

As significant differences emerged in the two classes in the delivery of the interdisciplinary project, the next section will make a comparison.

6.3 A Comparison Between the Interdisciplinary Project in the Two Classes

Based on the results of the member checks, Table 6.1 makes a comparison between the two interdisciplinary projects carried out in class A and B.

The first difference is the building to be designed. While in class A it was the canteen with the apartment of the keeper, in class B the object was a canteen with a parking underneath. According to the class B's Design teacher who made the decision to add the underground parking, the location was too central to avoid a parking facility. The effort was therefore to keep the project realistic, but during the discussion, students and other teachers agreed that this choice increased the degree of complexity in the project, to a point that was hardly manageable by the students. Many students consequently made serious mistakes when designing the canteen with the parking lot underneath it. By way of contrast, the class A's project was simple enough to be achievable by the students.

The second difference is the time span to develop the interdisciplinary project within the design subject (a major of the course). In class A, the Design teacher used the interdisciplinary project to teach other related topics, thus making a year-round topic. In doing so, all the curricula became more realistic and therefore more competence based. By way of contrast, in class B the Design teacher chose to dedicate only a semester to it and continued with the regular programme, which is more knowledge based, in the second semester. For the Design teacher, this mixed approach

Table 6.1 Comparison between the interdisciplinary projects as carried out in class A and B

	Class A	Class B
Object	Canteen with house of the keeper	Canteen with underground parking
Time dedicated to the interdisciplinary project in major subject	Whole year	One semester
Survey in the field	At the beginning of the school year	Almost at the end of the school year
Selection of the components for group work in major subject	made by the teacher	made by the students
Assessment types	Summative	summative and formative

was better to ensure that he covered all the topics so that the students would be better prepared for the state exam.

The third difference comes from the time of the year where the related field survey was carried out. In class A, the topography teacher went with the class at the beginning of the year, thus handing timely data for Design. In class B, the topography teacher chose to start the school year with the regular curriculum, and only towards the end of the year, when some time was left, did he send the students for the survey on the field. This choice partially hampered the initial phase of design, where students had to rely on incomplete data. Consequently, the coordination between subjects resulted better in class A.

The selection of the students for group work in Design was also different. In class A, it was done by the teacher after having weighted variables such as the initial blueprint and the students' performance. In so doing, the groups were balanced and heterogeneous. In class B the students made groups autonomously, which led to homogeneous groups basing on performance and liking. As a consequence for that, in-class group work in class A worked better.

The assessment forms were also different; in class A, it was only summative, therefore the students were not given intermediate feedback on their projects. In class B, the evaluation was both summative and formative, with the teacher mentoring the groups regularly. A competence-based approach would call for a mix of formative and summative assessment methods, therefore class B was better delivered according to a competence-based approach.

Overall, in class A, the interdisciplinary project transformed the curriculum into competence based, especially in the design subject. The project was delivered throughout the school year and embedded other related topics, it entailed productive in-class group work, and coordination among subjects worked better. More formative assessment forms would, however, be needed. In class B, the interdisciplinary project allowed only for a partial switch to a competence-based approach for half a year, and in-class group work and coordination between subjects did not work so well.

6.4 The Interdisciplinary Project Facing a Tertiary Contradiction

This section summarises the current implementation of the Interdisciplinary project from a Cultural Historical Activity Theory point of view. A new form of activity develops through the resolution of contradictions (Engeström, 2015; Virkkunen & Newnham, 2013). When the new model is implemented in the activity, system changes are necessary for the elements of the activity to make the new object, with different tools, rules, division of labour and community. In tertiary contradictions, the implementation of the new model causes tensions between the present form and the application of the new model in the elements of the activity system. In this

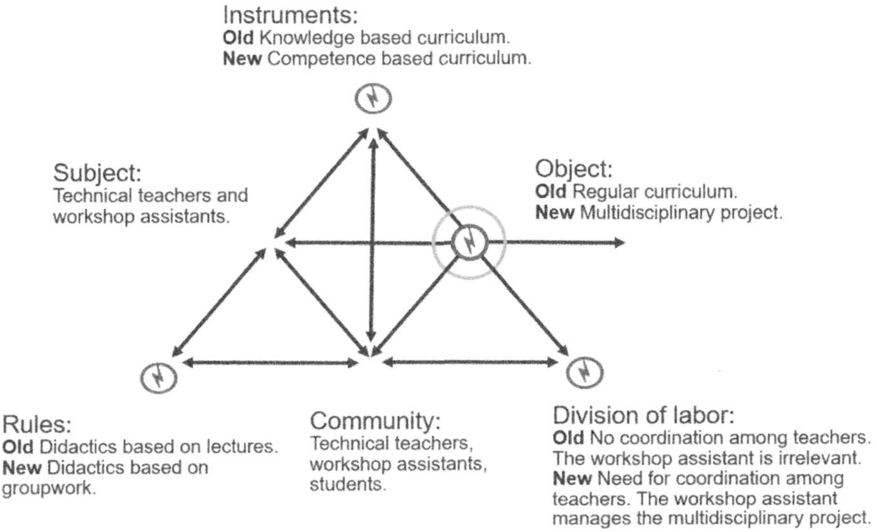

Fig. 6.1 Tertiary contradiction illustrated in the triangular model of activity

research, the application of the interdisciplinary project provokes a tertiary contradiction which is visible: (1) in the tensions between the old and the new curriculum; (2) in the tensions between the old and coordination among teachers and between teachers and workshop assistants; (3) in the tensions between the old didactics and the new didactics. Figure 6.1 depicts the tertiary contradiction pervading the elements of the activity system.

6.5 Old and New Curriculum

The emergence of a shared interdisciplinary project has shown tensions between the old and the new curriculum; on the one hand, there is the knowledge-based curriculum, and on the other, there is the interdisciplinary project that is competence based. Three different points of view illustrate such tensions in the object: a Design teacher teaching his subject with the new concept, one topography teacher teaching the course programme the customary way, and a Design teacher who teaches half of the year with the new concept and half of the year in the customary way.

Firstly, the Class A's Design teacher argues that he found it a good idea to expand the interdisciplinary project at the expenses of the regular school programmes based on knowledge:

192	*Facilitator*	*In the Grade A class, the teacher could employ the whole school year for the interdisciplinary project, and could therefore deepen it more. In doing so, he abandoned the disciplinary aspects of design, didn't you (turning to Design teacher 3)?*
193	*Design teacher 3*	*Yes, indeed!*
194	*Design teacher 2*	*Well, I dealt only with the interdisciplinary project during first semester*
195	*Facilitator*	*I remember this difference*
196	*Design teacher 3*	*What I reckon is that in the school program there are many things that have a limited use (for working life)*

Second, the class B's topography teacher solved this dilemma by choosing the old curriculum:

326	*Topography teacher 2*	*If we chose an approach fully competence-based since the beginning of the school year, this would have a price to be paid. If we want to deal with concrete problems such as the PREGEO procedure, it is clear that we have to reduce all the classic topics of topography including the street project. We cannot deal with everything in our course programs. In my case, I tried to reach a compromise; I did not give up the kernel of my regular school program, and understood the interdisciplinary project only as a plus for the students*

For topography teacher 2, the interdisciplinary project was just a positive element to be dealt with as an added value of the regular course programme.

Third, in between the two points of view there is class B's Design teacher:

327	*Design teacher 2*	*The program dictated by the Ministry of Education has been important for me. I discussed with the class on this issue, and eventually we came up with the solution to perform the interdisciplinary project during the first semester, and to dedicate the second semester for the regular school program to, thus preparing the students for the state exam*

The Ministry of Education's programme and the state exam are mentioned as justifications to remain anchored to a knowledge-based view of surveying.

6.5.1 The Old and New Coordination Among Teaching Staff

The implementation of the new concept caused a tension in the division of labour between teachers and workshop assistants. Historically, workshop assistants are a product of the latest school reform of 2007 and have appeared in schools since

2012. Their role of technical and practical assistants would be to assist the teachers during both workshops and lessons. From the teachers' point of view, however, their function is yet to be found. In the old way of teaching based on knowledge and lectures, workshop assistants are unnecessary. In the implementation of the new concept, they become valuable as they are in charge of liaising the technical subjects and coordinate the subject teachers around the interdisciplinary project. Similarly, the coordination between subjects is also important, as the survey on the field by the topography teacher had been carried out first to give the students the idea of the site where the building will have to be designed.

6.5.2 Tensions Between the Old and the New Didactics

The new concept calls for new rules concerning class didactics, especially in the design subject. While the old curriculum makes use of lectures, the interdisciplinary project requires more workload for students because they consider the many constraints in the field necessary when designing realistic blueprints. Group work becomes therefore necessary to share the workload, but the Design teachers find it hard to set the rules for it. Although the students did not rose the problem of group work during the third follow-up workshop, there have been issues for both classes, especially in the coordination of the homework. While teachers contend that in-class group work runs smoothly, at home there are two problems. Firstly, some students do not hand the work by the established deadline, thus hampering the work of their colleagues who base their work on that output. Second, sometimes one group member does not perform the task at all, and another student who has been allocated with them does the job. The teachers will therefore have to find tools and rules to better organise group work among students to improve the implementation of the new concept.

Another follow-up workshop was carried out close to the end of the school year, and the teaching staff decided to continue the development of the interdisciplinary project the following year. It is already positive news that the new concept is continuing despite the obstacles faced, and the teaching staff is showing their sense of initiative and entrepreneurship not to give up in their endeavour. In order for the interdisciplinary project to be better implemented, the tensions above will have to be overcome, and the participants will need to decide what still has to be learnt to deliver it more effectively, according to a fully competence-based approach. This approach must include: use of formative assessment; personalisation of the programme according to the students' needs; integration of assessment with forms of self-assessment and reflection; connection within the school activities and between outer school activities and integration of knowledge, skills and attitudes.

This chapter discussed from a CHAT point of view how the expansive learning process is developing. While the Change Laboratory caused a medium-sized cycle of expansive learning with a new concept to be progressively put into practice, the participants strive to progress in the macro-cycle by solving contradictions, to make the interdisciplinary project the customary way to teach surveying in Grade 5. During the implementation of the new concept, they face issues they had not envisioned when designed it, and by solving them, they stabilise the activity and make it the customary way to work. Building on this chapter, Chap. 7 draws conclusions on the Change Laboratory for teacher training in entrepreneurial education. It will show the extent to which the implementation of the new concept is being effective for solving the original challenge for which the Change Laboratory was held, that is how to improve the number of enrolments in surveying.

Bibliography

Biggs, J., & Tang, C. (2011). *Teaching for quality learning at university. What the student does*. New York: McGraw-Hill.

Engeström, Y. (2001). Expansive learning at work: Toward an activity theoretical reconceptualization. *Journal of Education and Work, 14*(1), 133–156.

Engeström, Y. (2015). *Learning by expanding*. Cambridge University Press.

Engeström, Y., & Sannino, A. (2010). Studies of expansive learning: Foundations, findings and future challenges. *Educational Research Review, 5*(1), 1–24.

Engeström, Y., Virkkunen, J., Helle, M., Pihlaja, J., & Poikela, R. (1996). The change laboratory as a tool for transforming work. *Lifelong Learning in Europe, 1*(2), 10–17.

Johnson, D. W., & Johnson, R. T. (1999). Making cooperative learning work. *Theory into Practice, 38*(2), 67–73.

Koenen, A.-K., Dochy, F., & Berghmans, I. (2015). A phenomenographic analysis of the implementation of competence-based education in higher education. *Teaching and Teacher Education, 50*, 1–12.

Marton, F. (2014). *Necessary conditions of learning*. New York: Routledge.

Merriam, S. B. (2009). *Qualitative Research: A guide to design and Implementation*. Somerset, NJ: Jossey-Bass.

Ravitch, S. M., & Carl, N. M. (2015). *Qualitative research: Bridging the conceptual, theoretical, and methodological*. Los Angeles: SAGE Publications.

Sturing, L., Biemans, H. J., Mulder, M., & De Bruijn, E. (2011). The nature of study programmes in vocational education: evaluation of the model for comprehensive competence-based vocational education in the Netherlands. *Vocations and Learning, 4*(3), 191–210.

Virkkunen, J., & Newnham, D. S. (2013). *The Change Laboratory. A tool for Collaborative Development of Work and Education*. Rotterdam: Sense.

Young, M. (2001). Contextualizing a new approach to learning: Some comments on Yrjo Engestrom's theory of expansive learning. *Journal of Education and Work, 14*(1), 157–161.

Open Access This chapter is licensed under the terms of the Creative Commons Attribution 4.0 International License (http://creativecommons.org/licenses/by/4.0/), which permits use, sharing, adaptation, distribution and reproduction in any medium or format, as long as you give appropriate credit to the original author(s) and the source, provide a link to the Creative Commons license and indicate if changes were made.

The images or other third party material in this chapter are included in the chapter's Creative Commons license, unless indicated otherwise in a credit line to the material. If material is not included in the chapter's Creative Commons license and your intended use is not permitted by statutory regulation or exceeds the permitted use, you will need to obtain permission directly from the copyright holder.

Chapter 7
Conclusions: Towards Entrepreneurial Education Through the Change Laboratory

Abstract This conclusive chapter argues that the Change Laboratory intervention has an impact on the teaching staff, the students and the organisation, the role of the management being key in sustaining the change effort. A Change Laboratory intervention develops initiative and entrepreneurship in the teaching staff, both through its outcomes and during the formative process itself. Firstly, the outcome of Change Laboratory can be a new concept, and its implementation brings a renewal of pedagogy. The eventual result is to integrate entrepreneurship into the core of the school, as this change in teaching practice creates value. Second, the process of participation in the Change Laboratory causes the development of the teaching staff's collective transformative agency, changing the focus of discourse from criticising the state of things and blaming others, to committing to implement a coordinated multidisciplinary project with new didactics. The participation process has also caused a switch from individual to collective actions. The Change Laboratory, therefore, demonstrates that entrepreneurship becomes a collective and social phenomenon where individuals face a problem that threatens their community. They take the lead and find a solution that creates value for themselves and their community. With the Change Laboratory for teachers in-service training, new ideas of pedagogical practices are transformed into collective action and value. This view of entrepreneurship emphasises the dimension of the sense of initiative and entrepreneurship as key competence for participation, citizenship and personal fulfilment, which provide the foundations for a New Skills Agenda.

Keywords Entrepreneurial education · Change Laboratory · Teacher training
Collective transformative agency · Interdisciplinary project
Sense of initiative and entrepreneurship

This chapter seeks to answer to the research question formulated in Chap. 1, and it is divided in four sections. While the first section summarises the content of the previous chapters, the second looks at the impact of the Change Laboratory. This goal is achieved by analysing the figures of pre-enrolments from 2015 to 2018, and by reviewing the changes that took place in the teaching staff, in the programme and in the institution. The impact on the teaching staff, the focus of this Change Laboratory

© The Author(s) 2019

D. Morselli, *The Change Laboratory for Teacher Training in Entrepreneurship Education*, SpringerBriefs in Education,
https://doi.org/10.1007/978-3-030-02571-7_7

intervention, is analysed by looking at the changes in the five characteristics of the SIE interview described in Chap. 2. The impact on the programme and therefore on students is visible in the new didactics, a competence approach preparing teachers more effectively for work and giving them more participation in terms of decision-making. The leadership was structured to support the teachers' sense of initiative and entrepreneurship.

The third section seeks to answer to the research question put forward in Chap. 1. This research explores the extent to which a Change Laboratory intervention as in-service training can be useful for promoting a sense of initiative and entrepreneurship among the teaching staff. This part of the chapter argues that the Change Laboratory develops the teaching staff's sense of initiative and entrepreneurship in the outcome and in the process. The outcome of a Change Laboratory can be a new concept for their collective activity, and the implementation of the new concept leads to a pedagogical renewal in the teaching practices. Through a interdisciplinary project, this Change Laboratory intervention ensured a switch towards a competence-based approach to teach surveying. This transformation created value for the school, the creation of value being a core element for entrepreneurship. The impact on the process can be found in the participants' development of a collective transformative agency, from criticising and blaming to commitment and implementation of the new concept. While a top-down approach determines resistance in teachers who become the executors of policy recommendations, bottom-up approaches, especially formative interventions, are designed to help develop and express collective transformative agency—with the participants tackling important issues that can only be solved by a cooperative action. The fourth section draws final conclusions. With the shift of the unit of analysis from the individual to a collective activity system, the Change Laboratory sheds new light on entrepreneurial education for a new skills Agenda.

7.1 The Story so Far

Skills, a term used to indicate what an individual can do, understand and know, are a path to prosperity and employability. Within the 'A new Skills Agenda for Europe', the European Commission (2016) has launched a revision of key competences, and special interest will be given to the promotion of entrepreneurial and innovation-oriented mindsets. In the literature, there is a polysemy around the term entrepreneurship education. Consistent with the literature (Lackeus, 2015), in this study entrepreneurial education is the general term embedding the others (such as enterprise and entrepreneurship education), and a sense of initiative and entrepreneurship is a European key competence for lifelong learning. It deals with turning ideas into action (European Commission, 2007), and it represents the outcome for entrepreneurial education.

When designing and delivering a course in entrepreneurial education, there should be a coherence between the learning outcomes, the activities of teaching and learning and the assessment practices (QAA, 2018). Assessment is defined as an educational practice serving to fill the gap between the desired outcomes and what the student has achieved. Not only assessment is essential to promote learning in students, but it also allows teachers to reflect on and enhance their programmes (Biggs & Tang, 2011). Drawing on both literatures of key competencies and entrepreneurship education and training, the assessment of a sense of initiative and entrepreneurship cannot be a 'one size fits all' process, but should be a programme tailored to the requirements of the institution and the environment, with the active collaboration of the stakeholders. In the case of teacher evaluation, the Sense of Initiative and Entrepreneurship questionnaire seeks to measure how secondary teachers educate for the key competence of the sense of initiative and entrepreneurship as cross-curricular subject (Morselli, 2017). Any teacher could, therefore, educate for a sense of initiative and entrepreneurship while teaching their subject. One possible way to implement this strategy is by teachers role modelling for students what entrepreneurship looks like in their teaching practice (European Commission, 2014; Penaluna, Penaluna, Usei, & Griffiths, 2015). The Sense of Initiative and Entrepreneurship questionnaire was administered to the teachers and workshop assistants who later participated in the Change Laboratory. Results suggested that the teaching staff would need help to gain a sense of initiative and entrepreneurship to cross the boundaries between disciplines, the boundaries between school and work, as well as apply active didactics coupled with diverse forms of assessment.

A theory of entrepreneurship calls for a theory of learning, and most of the literature on entrepreneurship relies on Kolb's (1984) theory of experiential learning. This theory has issues, for example it was initially developed as an inventory, and it is based on a cycle that is not theoretically grounded (Morselli, Costa, & Margiotta, 2014). Another theory of adult learning is necessary to back entrepreneurship, and this can be expansive learning, a theory of innovation and collective change of practices where practitioners learn something that is not yet there (Engeström, 2015). The unit of analysis includes a collective activity system mediated by artefacts and oriented to an object; such system is studied in its network of relationships with the other activity systems (Engeström, 2001). An activity system is characterised by a community of individuals with diverse points of view. Yet to understand its present form and its possibilities, a historical perspective is essential, since within this lens contradictions can be recognised, such as the accumulated structural tensions within and between activity systems. These elements play a key role in expansive transformation of the activity system itself. A school course can be studied as an activity system, the object being the students' learning. Formative interventions, especially the Change Laboratory, are designed to trigger cycles of expansive learning, and are based on two principles, 'double stimulation' and 'ascending from the abstract to the concrete' (Sannino, Engeström, & Lemos, 2016). The Change Laboratory is suited for activity systems facing a major challenge; it is characterised by a highly mediating setting with writing surfaces used according to different levels of abstraction and to an historical perspective (Virkkunen & Newnham, 2013). Other important features of the Change Laboratory are a dialectical movement between distanced intellectual analysis and close emotional involvement, and the mirrors, videotaped materials gathered on the field useful to trigger discussion.

A course in surveying in an Italian secondary technical institute was chosen for the research because it had suffered from a dramatic loss of students in recent years.

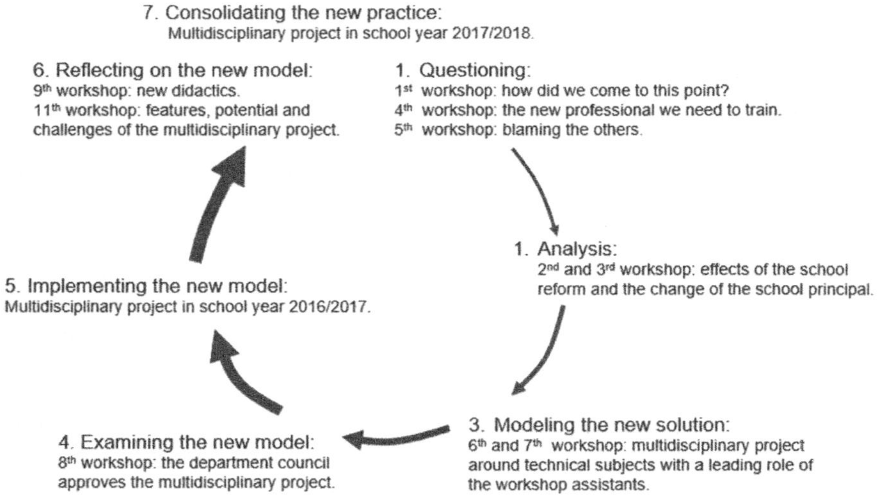

Fig. 7.1 Expansive learning process during and after the Change Laboratory intervention

Moreover, the teaching staff had not fully understood the changes in surveying that had taken place with the school reform and after almost 10 years were still training for the pre-reform surveyor, with a curriculum centred on the construction of new buildings. Instead, the school reform and the market transformations had called for a switch from the construction of new to the renovation of the old, the green skills and the management of the territory. The new concept developed during the Change Laboratory workshops is that in the two Grade 5 classes, 3 technical teachers for each class would teach around a common and realistic interdisciplinary project concerning the construction of a new building in an area close to the school. The realistic and hands-on interdisciplinary project would be carried out around traditional technical topics, allowing students to make connections and understand deeply the core concepts of surveying. It was intended to be coordinated by the workshop assistants who liaise the subjects.

Figure 7.1 summarises the expansive learning triggered by the Change Laboratory intervention. Under each expansive learning action, there is the workshop where it was dealt with and the outcome. The expansive learning process continues outside the 11 Change Laboratory workshops with the implementation of the interdisciplinary project in school year 2016/2017 (5th action) and its consolidation in 2017/2018 (7th action).

Described in the words of the participants—teachers, students and workshop assistants—the new concept has features, potential and challenges, but has also historical antecedents. The senior teachers implemented a similar project when it was a mandatory activity carried out during specifically allocated hours before the school reform. However, a new professional figure, the workshop assistant, now helps connect the diverse subjects into a whole. Additionally, the project requires a competence-based approach and students' group work. These elements distinguish the interdisciplinary project from the projects carried out at the end of the 1990s. According to the teachers, the project features are that it is based on realistic tasks and problems, it connects diverse technical subject matters and allows students to work in groups. The interdisciplinary project also has diverse transformative potentials: it can change the state exam based on a competence; it calls for an evaluation system beyond knowledge towards competence; it can change the curriculum to make it more up to date; through its advertisement on the school open day it has the potential to attract enrolments; and through group work it fights bullying and promotes group work as an important skill set for working life. The interdisciplinary project also faces challenges: it is more multidisciplinary than interdisciplinary; the role of workshop assistants is not fully utilised because of the high turnover and lack of experience; and it could result in an excessive workload for students.

The findings of this analysis were used as a starting point during the third follow-up. From one perspective, this workshop served for validating the research findings. From another perspective, the tasks served to trigger the expansive learning action of reflecting on and evaluating the process, to think what else needed to be learnt for the better implementation of the interdisciplinary the following school year. The participants in the follow-up workshop—teachers, workshop assistants and students—confirm they now see the interdisciplinary project as based on group work, real tasks, and connecting the technical disciplines. This development demonstrates a move from a knowledge-based approach to competence-based approach, as well as giving a holistic perspective of surveying. A drawback concerns the workshop assistants whose connecting role is underestimated. Given the importance that the participants attribute to teaching the interdisciplinary project according to a competence-based approach, the second task of the follow-up was to, with grids, evaluate the extent with which the interdisciplinary project had been delivered according to a competence-based approach. Compared with the students' point of view, the teachers tended to overestimate the degree they teach the interdisciplinary through a competence-based approach.

In CHAT terms such tension between teaching for knowledge and teaching for competence is a manifestation of a tertiary contradiction. New forms of activity develop through the resolution of contradictions, and in tertiary contradictions, the implementation of the new model causes tensions between the present form and the application of the new model in the elements of the activity system (Virkkunen & Newnham, 2013). In this research, the application of the interdisciplinary project provokes a tertiary contradiction which is visible: in the tensions between the old and the new objects, with a curriculum delivered, respectively, according to a knowledge-based and a competence-based approach; in the tensions between the old and new division of labour (which is a significant factor in coordination between teachers, as well as between teachers and workshop assistants); and in the tensions between the old and new rules (for example in the old and new didactics, respectively, students in the class working alone or in groups). The resolution of this contradiction will allow the advancement through the expansive learning process with a interdisciplinary approach delivered according to a fully competence-based approach.

7.2 Impact of the Change Laboratory Workshops

This section deals with the impact of the workshops on the student enrolments, the teaching staff, the students already in the school, and the organisation. The European Commission (2014) defines impact as observable changes at different levels (individual, organisational, societal) as a direct consequence of an educational activity. The observable changes can be qualitative or qualitative. Concerning quantity, this Change Laboratory was set to help the teaching staff tackle the diminished number of enrolments. Table 7.1 shows the pre-enrolments in surveying from the school year 2015–2016 to 2017–2018, two years the interdisciplinary project has been running.

In the Italian school system pre-enrolments are a better indicator than the actual enrolments, because they allow for a more effective appraisal of a school's attractiveness to future students. Enrolments also include the students who failed Grade 1 and simply repeated it, and this figure can vary. The pre-enrolments of the school year 2015–2016 correspond to the school year when the Change Laboratory was held. However, follow-up workshops were held regularly to sustain the expansive learning process. Overall, the number of students in surveying has been growing since the Change Laboratory workshops. During the Change laboratory, the participants discussed how to better promote surveying outside the school, for example with better organised open days. The interdisciplinary project could be used to promote the course as a unique opportunity featured at the school during both open days and through the students' word of mouth about their experiences. Beyond improvement of freshmen, however, there have been qualitative changes in the way teachers educate for a sense of initiative and entrepreneurship, in the students' achievement of outcomes with changes in the curriculum, as well as at the organisational level.

Firstly, the five dimensions of the SIE interview on the entrepreneurial teacher described in the second chapter can help show the impact of the Change Laboratory on the teaching staff. The first characteristic of entrepreneurial educators is that they embed into their course a selection of learning outcomes of the sense of initiative and entrepreneurship and make use of an appropriate mix of assessment forms, and teachers have not yet moved in this direction. The second feature, however, is a focus on active pedagogies, and the design teachers, a major subject in surveying, have extensively made use of group work and project-based work to deliver their courses, even though with the tensions mentioned in the previous chapter. The third characteristic is educating for entrepreneurial attitudes, and during the Change Laboratory the teachers have repeatedly discussed the student's attitudes, especially initiative and autonomy, and how to educate for them. There is an increasing awareness that they should educate for the entrepreneurial attitudes that are important for the surveyor. The fourth characteristic is to connect across the boundaries between disciplines within the school, as well as those between the school and the outside world. While

Table 7.1 Pre-enrolments in the school before and after the Change Laboratory intervention

School year/course	Surveying
2015–2016	27
2016–2017	32
2017–2018	29
2018–2019	37

to some extent the teaching staff already crossed the boundaries between school and the outside world with school visits and surveying in the field, the major contribution of the interdisciplinary project is that they started crossing the boundaries between their disciplines by organising a interdisciplinary project that was coordinated by the workshop assistants. The fifth feature of the entrepreneurial teacher is to be entrepreneurial in a lifelong learning perspective, both inside and outside the school environments and throughout their professional development. Rather than being a specific course on entrepreneurship education, the Change Laboratory sought to develop the teachers' collective sense of initiative and entrepreneurship. Due to an increased awareness of the importance of school open days which was discussed during the Change Laboratory, surveying teachers and their workshop assistants are also taking better care in how their course is presented during the open days. They also advertise their interdisciplinary project as flagship initiative. Before the Change Laboratory, the teaching staff was blaming other factors for the drop in the enrolments the course had suffered from. After it had taken place, the surveying teaching staff has taken the lead to change its circumstances. Such increased sense of initiative and entrepreneurship is the most important outcome of the Change Laboratory intervention and will be further discussed in the following section.

Concerning the impact of the Change Laboratory on students, this development can be seen in terms of new didactics, in a curriculum delivered according to a competence-based approach, and in their increased participation in the decision-making processes. One of the effects of the interdisciplinary project has been a switch from lectures to active didactics such as group work, which is recognised as one the outcomes for entrepreneurship education (Bacigalupo, Kampylis, Punie, & Brande, 2016). Students have known more about cooperation and rules to make a group work effective and have acquired more autonomy. This conclusion is in line with Haara and Jenssen (2016), who contend that pedagogical entrepreneurship should move beyond business creation towards human development with an emphasis on authentic activities, action and self-regulation. For Draycott and Rae (2011), enterprise education can be simply considered a way of solving the long-standing gap between education and the work of work, and this area has been the objective of the interdisciplinary project. This study shows how students learnt *through* entrepreneurship rather than *about* entrepreneurship.

Another observable change in students caused by the Change Laboratory has been an increased participation in the process of decision-making. Through in-class focus groups with teachers, discussions and participation in the follow-up workshop, students have made their voice heard on the potentials and threats of the interdisciplinary project, but also on the didactics such as group work. This is in line with Dal, Elo, Leffler, Svedberg, and Westerberg (2016), who suggest that pedagogical entrepreneurship is useful to develop new and emancipatory pedagogies which lie in contrast to more strict approaches to learning and teaching.

Concerning the impact of the Change Laboratory at the organisational level, I interviewed the school director asking for the changes she could observe, and she pointed out three types of effects. Firstly, teachers have gotten far more active in promoting their courses during the school open days. The result has been an improvement in pre-enrolments not only in surveying, but also in the other courses. Second, the school director perceived an improvement of the image of the school outside. This has been communicated by privileged observers, institutions and journalists with sentences such as "We know your school goes above and beyond" or "In delivering work experience you are the best". Third, the school director reports an increased sense of initiative and entrepreneurship from the teaching staff. It was the surveying teachers who autonomously implemented the interdisciplinary project. Now the school's young teaching staff turn to her with more trust and the will to cooperate, a condition for pedagogical entrepreneurship (Ruskovaara, Hämäläinen, & Pihkala, Ruskovaara et al. 2016), and before the Change Laboratory the situation was quite different.

At the organisational level the CL has left a mark on the course of surveying, which has started acting with a sense of initiative and entrepreneurship: to promote it and to improve it. Before the Change Laboratory, the teaching staff was blaming the others (the school director, the course in graphics, the students and parents, etcetera) for the drop in the enrolments the course had suffered from. After the Change Laboratory, the surveying teaching staff has taken the lead to change their course's circumstances. The role of the school management has been to create the conditions for the teaching staff to take initiatives to revitalise their course in surveying; the issue was how to call surveying teachers and workshop assistants for action. In this Change Laboratory process, the role of school management, especially the vice director and the school director, has been of help and interest. From one perspective, the vice director took part to each workshop and was determined to set the method to develop the new concept. He came with a written idea of interdisciplinary project, and he proposed to start discussing it to find the best concrete solution possible. From another perspective, the school director promoted the research with the organisation of the launch events in the school. It was she who suggested that the surveying course could receive most benefit from the formative intervention. However, although she was kept informed on the outcomes of the workshops, she never made pressures on the participants allowing an autonomy among her staff in the end, even when some of the participants (in the historical analysis) criticised her for having chosen in 2010 to run new courses in the school. When the participants had conceived the new idea, she participated in the workshop to help implement the interdisciplinary project according to the school regulations and the available resources. Coherently with formative interventions where it is the participants who take the lead (Engeström, 2011), the task of the management has not been to tell the teachers what they could do, but support them in their change effort which was led by them. This approach encouraged characteristic attitudes of entrepreneurial education such as autonomy, risk-taking and experimentation.

7.3 A Double View of Entrepreneurial Education in the Process and in the Outcome

This research sought to explore the extent which a Change Laboratory intervention as in-service training can be useful for promoting a sense of initiative and entrepreneurship among the teaching staff. The research question was:

"To what extent can a Change Laboratory help the teaching staff turn ideas into actions?" (RQ1).

The expression "to turn ideas into action" represents the definition of a sense of initiative and entrepreneurship as from the European Commission (2007). It is maintained that by showing a sense of initiative and entrepreneurship in the school, the teaching staff will act as role model for their students, as argued extensively in the literature (European Commission, 2014; Heinonen & Poikkijoki, 2006; Penaluna et al., 2015; Ruskovaara & Pihkala, 2015).

Following the analysis of the section on the impact above, this chapter argues that the Change Laboratory has a double effect on the teachers' sense of initiative and entrepreneurship, in the outcomes and the process.

- The outcome of a Change Laboratory can be a new object and concept for their collective activity (Engeström & Sannino, 2010). In this research, the new concept has been a interdisciplinary project. The consequence in this case was a pedagogical renewal in the teaching practices: competence-based approaches with structured group work and assessment forms, with a central role of workshop assistants. As it has been displayed in the impact of the research above, the new concept has undoubtedly created value for the organisation and the students, and value creation—which can be either economic, social and cultural—represents the common core of entrepreneurship and the goal for entrepreneurial education (Lackeus, 2015). Furthermore, Peltonen (2015) analysed the pedagogical side of entrepreneurship and argued that teachers see entrepreneurial education as resulting in pedagogical renewal and professional development. In this study, the Change laboratory has brought pedagogical renewal with the teaching of a interdisciplinary project, which carried the need for their professional development towards a competence-based approach to teaching. Hence, rather than becoming the recipients of linear interventions and policy recommendations, with the Change Laboratory the teaching staff collectively chose what they thought they should learn to innovate their practices.
- The second way with which the teaching staff have developed a sense of initiative and entrepreneurship stems from the *process*. The participation in the Change Laboratory allows for the emergence and development of collective transformative agency, which is defined as "breaking away from the given frame of action and take the initiative to transform it" (Virkkunen, 2006, p. 49). Throughout the workshops, the participants shifted from criticising the state of things, to blaming others, to committing to teach a coordinated interdisciplinary project with new didactics. Simultaneously, they moved from individual to collective initiatives. Before the intervention they taught their subject, as it was separate from the other subjects in the school, and they complained about the lack of cooperation. In order to implement the new concept, the teaching staff had to work collectively to incorporate a common topic within the context of their classroom.

It can, thus, be concluded that *with the Change Laboratory for teachers in-service training, new ideas of pedagogical practices are transformed into collective action and value.* This definition embeds the double effect of the Change Laboratory in creating the conditions for the development of the teachers' sense of initiative and entrepreneurship. That is, in the product with the implementation of new pedagogical practices that create value for the school, and in the process with the development of their collective transformative agency. Opposed to linear interventions, formative interventions set the stage for the participants to take the lead of the learning process. Since teachers are also citizens, they must learn and display these competencies for both themselves and their students (Gordon et al., 2009), and this approach is made possible through the Change Laboratory intervention. Similar to the students, the teaching staff learnt *through* entrepreneurship rather than *about* entrepreneurship (Haara and Jenssen, 2016).

One of the curiosities of this study has been on how to document the outcomes of the Change Laboratory in the *process* that is the teaching staff's collective transformative agency. In the Change Laboratory, the consequential actions of change are mostly performed in vivo, after and between the workshops (Engeström, 2011). Agentive actions do not stand on their own, but can only be studied as contextualised in their activity system, while the individuals break away from the given frame of action and implement the new practices. Hence, the solution on how to make visible the participants' development of transformative agency was to show how the interdisciplinary project was conceived, how it breaks away from the old and it is being developed. It is the actions taken to overcome contradictions that materialise the teaching staff's collective transformative agency. By showing how a new object is generated and how participants strive for its progressive implementation, this study shows the participants' collective transformative agency. Translated into an educational language, it could be said that by *showing how an idea is being generated and collectively turned into action, this study shows the development of the participants' sense of initiative and entrepreneurship.*

There are, however, differences between a collective transformative agency in CHAT and a sense of initiative and entrepreneurship. The two terms come from different ontologies, and therefore should not be confused. Collective transformative agency stems from Vygotksian studies, while a sense of initiative and entrepreneurship was conceived within European educational policies. In an activity system, a collective transformative agency focuses on how the participants collectively break away from the given frame of action. In the case of a sense of initiative and entrepreneurship, the focus is on how innovative ideas are transformed into courses of action by the individual, thus creating value. Hence, a collective transformative agency focuses on the collective contribution of all individuals to their object, while a sense of initiative and entrepreneurship concentrates on the individual. Although it is the individual who displays and owns a sense of initiative and entrepreneurship, this attitude can also be collectively displayed during coordinated actions.

Learning a sense of initiative and entrepreneurship in the *process* and in the *outcome* is closely related to the two key processes of the Change Laboratory, double stimulation and concept formation. While Chap. 4 shows the chain of stimuli used for double stimulation in the workshops that develop in the participants a collective transformative agency, Chaps. 5 and 6 detail what the interdisciplinary project is like. Appendix A shows the interdisciplinary project as it was in April 2016, a two-page document entirely written by the participants with the description of contents, didactics and actors involved. While these chapters give an instantaneous picture of what the interdisciplinary project is like in the specific historical movement, during the implementation the new concept is constantly evolving and being improved. During the school year 2017–2018, for example, the teaching staff selected a different area with a different project to be designed, a gas station. They also changed the way student group work was carried out in the class with smaller groups, and better coordinated their subjects and the role of the workshop assistants.

7.4 Concluding Remarks. Towards Teacher Training in Entrepreneurship with the Change Laboratory

Agency is a relevant mediator of educational change (Kumpulainen, Kajamaa, & Rajala, 2018). Change Laboratory are advisable when organisations are facing major transformations, and nobody knows what needs to be learnt (Engestrom & Sannino, 2010). The Change Laboratory is characterised as a bottom-up approach, where the change effort is initiated and led by the participants, with the participants tackling issues key for the organisation and that can only be solved by a cooperative effort. It should also be considered that, as they are remediating environments, Change Laboratory workshops are open-ended processes, and the outcomes cannot be determined at the beginning. An example is that the teachers set into use the concept of competence instead of entrepreneurship, but this should not be seen at odds with the aim of this study. Firstly, formative interventions are guided and led by the participants, therefore the researcher's task is to facilitate the change effort rather than imposing their agenda or own concepts. Second, although the participants admitted during the workshops that they had been forced by the school reforms to move to competence in their curricula without never being trained on competence-based education, this concept was much more familiar than entrepreneurship. Third, as I noted in Chap. 1, the model of Sturing, Biemans, Mulder, and De Bruijn (2011), which was used in the eleventh workshop, has extraordinary similarities with pedagogical entrepreneurship. It is centred on authentic projects that are inspired by 'in the world out there', cooperation among teachers and lifelong learning skills such as reflection and citizenship.

As a new concept, the interdisciplinary project has been a way to transcend the dialectics between old and new pedagogies. Likewise, learning environments and other concepts introduced in education (Engeström, 2009), competence could become a static generalisation of little use if not contextualised appropriately. Rather than teaching for competence for the sake of doing so, the Change Laboratory workshops allowed the teaching staff to fill this concept with meaning and to make it relevant for their context.

This research has been characterised by a double thread: the tensions between formative and linear interventions, and the tensions between policy documents on entrepreneurship and how entrepreneurship is actually enacted and taught by educators. Concerning the first tension between formative and linear interventions, this study explains their possible circular relationship: best practices lead to emerging practices, which in turn can become best practices. The SIE interview displays the strengths and weaknesses of teachers that can be tackled through a formative intervention. During the Change Laboratory, the teachers designed a interdisciplinary project which was implemented the following school year in 2016/2017, and an improved version was delivered in 2017/2018, thus becoming a flagship in the school. This suggests a possible circularity between linear interventions—producing best practices, and formative interventions—producing emerging practices that later become best practices. Regarding the second thread on the tensions between the concept of entrepreneurship education as it is described in policy documents and how it is conceived and implemented by educators, this research suggests that the teaching staff can teach *through* entrepreneurship, that is by being entrepreneurial and change the course programme embedding pedagogical entrepreneurship, without necessarily knowing *about* entrepreneurship.

This study concentrated on understanding the interdisciplinary project and tracing the expansive learning cycle that led to the development of a new activity system. However, the data gathered in this research can be a springboard for future research such as understanding the development of agency both through double stimulation and relational agency:

- applying the model of Double Stimulation put forward by Sannino (2016) to the Change Laboratory workshops to analyse how the first stimuli and conflict of stimuli trigger auxiliary motives and volition;
- apply the concept of relation agency elaborated by Edwards (2011) to the workshops to study the way the participants cooperate to expand the object of their activity, how they recognise the motives and resources of the colleagues as they interpret the object, and align own responses to the improved interpretations;
- studying the principle of ascending from the abstract to the concrete, that is how a germ cell is developed into a fully operating concept (Sannino & Engeström, 2017);
- analysing the power relationships within the workshops (Ravitch & Carl, 2015).

With the shift of the unit of analysis from the individual to a collective activity system, the Change Laboratory sheds new light on entrepreneurial education. Entrepreneurship is not only an individualistic and economic phenomenon (Jones & Spicer, 2009; Kyro, 2006), and becomes a collective and social phenomenon where individuals face a problem that threatens their community. They take the lead of the situation and find a solution that creates value for themselves and their community. Notwithstanding the creation of value, entrepreneurship moves from business creation to tackling societal needs. In a similar vein, Bahri and Haftendorn (2006) suggested that the success of entrepreneurial education could indeed be measured by contributions to learning, to teaching practice, to poverty reduction and community improvement, and to more collective decision-making. This view of entrepreneurship encompasses the opposition between entrepreneurship as the lonely entrepreneur and intrapreneurship as employees being entrepreneurial within companies. In one sense, the division between these perspectives is because change does not start from an individual hero but is carried out by a collectiveness, with the activity system as unit of analysis. Notably, the management and the practitioners are not seen in opposition, but they rather cooperate to make change happen in a bottom-up change effort.

This view of entrepreneurship emphasises the dimension of the sense of initiative and entrepreneurship as key competence for participation, citizenship and personal fulfilment, for a new skills agenda in Europe.

Bibliography

Bacigalupo, M., Kampylis, P., Punie, Y., & Brande, G. V. D. (2016). *EntreComp: The entrepreneurship competence framework*. Brussels: Publication Office of the European Union.

Bahri, S., & Haftendorn, K. (2006). *Towards an Entrepreneurial Culture for the Twenty-first Century: Stimulating Entrepreneurial Spirit through Entrepreneurship Education in Secondary School*. Paris: UNESCO Publishing.

Biggs, J., & Tang, C. (2011). *Teaching for quality learning at university. What the student does*. New York: McGraw-Hill.

Dal, M., Elo, J., Leffler, E., Svedberg, G., & Westerberg, M. (2016). Research on pedagogical entrepreneurship–a literature review based on studies from Finland Iceland and Sweden. *Education Inquiry, 7*(2), 30036.

Draycott, M. C., & Rae, D. (2011). Enterprise education in schools and the role of competency frameworks. *International Journal of Entrepreneurial Behavior & Research, 17*(2), 127–145.

Edwards, A. (2011). Building common knowledge at the boundaries between professional practices: Relational agency and relational expertise in systems of distributed expertise. *International Journal of Educational Research, 50*(1), 33–39.

Engeström, Y. (2001). Activity theory as a framework for the study of organizational transformations. *Knowing in practice, February, 2001, University of Trento, Italy.*

Engeström, Y. (2009). From learning environments and implementation to activity systems and expansive learning.

Engeström, Y. (2011). From design experiments to formative interventions. *Theory & Psychology, 21*(5), 598–628.

Engeström, Y. (2015). *Learning by expanding*. Cambridge University Press.

Engeström, Y., & Sannino, A. (2010). Studies of expansive learning: Foundations, findings and future challenges. *Educational Research Review, 5*(1), 1–24.

European Commission. (2007). *European competences for lifelong learning*. Luxembourg: Publication Office of the European Union.

European Commission. (2014). *Entrepreneurship education. A guide for teachers*. Brussels: Unit entrepreneurship 2020.

European Commission. (2016). *A new skills agenda for Europe*. Retrieved from http://ec.europa.eu/social/main.jsp?catId=1223.

Gordon, J., Halász, G., Krawczyk, M., Leney, T., Michel, A., Pepper, D., ... Wiśniewski, J. (2009). *Key competences in Europe: Opening doors for lifelong learners across the school curriculum and teacher education*. In. Retrieved from http://www.case-research.eu/en/key-competences-in-europe-opening-doors-for-lifelong-learners-across-the-school-curriculum.

Haara, F. O., & Jenssen, E. S. (2016). Pedagogical entrepreneurship in teacher education–what and why? *Tímarit um uppeldi og menntun, 25*(2), 183–196.

Heinonen, J., & Poikkijoki, S.-A. (2006). An entrepreneurial-directed approach to entrepreneurship education: mission impossible? *Journal of Management Development, 25*(1), 80–94.

Jones, C., & Spicer, A. (2009). *Unmasking the entrepreneur*: Edward Elgar.

Kolb, D. A. (1984). *Experiential learning: experience as the source of learning and development Englewood Cliffs*. N.J.: Prentice-Hall.

Kumpulainen, K., Kajamaa, A., & Rajala, A. (2018). Understanding educational change: Agency-structure dynamics in a novel design and making environment. *Digital Education Review*(33), 26–38.

Kyro, P. (2006). Entrepreneurship education and Finnish society. Retrieved from http://www.researchgate.net/profile/Paula_Kyroe/publication/24137728_Entrepreneurship_Education_and_Finnish_Society/links/00b7d5343b20aab43b000000.pdf.

Lackeus, M. (2015). Entrepreneurship in Education. What, why, when, how. Retrieved from http://www.oecd.org/cfe/leed/BGP_Entrepreneurship-in-Education.pdf.

Morselli, D. (2017). *How do Italian vocational teachers educate for a sense of initiative and entrepreneurship?*. Development and initial application of the SIE questionnaire: Education + Training.

Morselli, D., Costa, M., & Margiotta, U. (2014). Entrepreneurship education based on the Change Laboratory. *The International Journal of Management Education, 12,* 333–348.

Peltonen, K. (2015). How can teachers' entrepreneurial competences be developed? A collaborative learning perspective. *Education + Training, 57*(5), 492–511.

Penaluna, K., Penaluna, A., Usei, C., & Griffiths, D. (2015). Enterprise education needs enterprising educators: A case study on teacher training provision. *Education + Training, 57*(8/9), 948–963.

QAA. (2018). *Enterprise and entrepreneurship education: Guidance for UK Higher Education Providers*. Gloucester: Quality Assurance Agency. Retrieved from www.qaa.ac.uk.

Ravitch, S. M., & Carl, N. M. (2015). *Qualitative research: Bridging the conceptual, theoretical, and methodological*. Los Angeles: SAGE Publications.

Ruskovaara, E., Hämäläinen, M., & Pihkala, T. (2016). HEAD teachers managing entrepreneurship education–Empirical evidence from general education. *Teaching and Teacher Education, 55,* 155–164.

Ruskovaara, E., & Pihkala, T. (2015). Entrepreneurship education in schools: empirical evidence on the teacher's role. *The Journal of Educational Research, 108*(3), 236–249.

Sannino, A. (2016). Double stimulation in the waiting experiment with collectives: Testing a Vygotskian model of the emergence of volitional action. *Integrative Psychological and Behavioral Science, 50*(1), 142–173.

Sannino, A., & Engeström, Y. (2017). Co-generation of societally impactful knowledge in Change Laboratories. *Management Learning, 48*(1), 80–96.

Sannino, A., Engeström, Y., & Lemos, M. (2016). Formative interventions for expansive learning and transformative agency. *Journal of the Learning Sciences, 25*(4), 599–633.

Sturing, L., Biemans, H. J., Mulder, M., & De Bruijn, E. (2011). The nature of study programmes in vocational education: evaluation of the model for comprehensive competence-based vocational education in the Netherlands. *Vocations and Learning, 4*(3), 191–210.

Virkkunen, J. (2006). Dilemmas in building shared transformative agency. Activités, 3(3-1).

Virkkunen, J., & Newnham, D. S. (2013). *The Change Laboratory. A tool for Collaborative Development of Work and Education*. Rotterdam: Sense.

Open Access This chapter is licensed under the terms of the Creative Commons Attribution 4.0 International License (http://creativecommons.org/licenses/by/4.0/), which permits use, sharing, adaptation, distribution and reproduction in any medium or format, as long as you give appropriate credit to the original author(s) and the source, provide a link to the Creative Commons license and indicate if changes were made.

The images or other third party material in this chapter are included in the chapter's Creative Commons license, unless indicated otherwise in a credit line to the material. If material is not included in the chapter's Creative Commons license and your intended use is not permitted by statutory regulation or exceeds the permitted use, you will need to obtain permission directly from the copyright holder.

Correction to: The Change Laboratory for Teacher Training in Entrepreneurship Education

Correction to:
D. Morselli, *The Change Laboratory for Teacher Training in Entrepreneurship Education*, SpringerBriefs in Education, https://doi.org/10.1007/978-3-030-02571-7

In the original version of the book, the funding information was missing. This has now been corrected.

The updated version of the book can be found at
https://doi.org/10.1007/978-3-030-02571-7

© The Author(s) 2019

D. Morselli, *The Change Laboratory for Teacher Training in Entrepreneurship Education*, SpringerBriefs in Education,
https://doi.org/10.1007/978-3-030-02571-7_8

Appendix A
The Interdisciplinary Project

Following the translation of the interdisciplinary project as discussed by the participants during the workshops.

Project proposal

For the course CET (construction, environment and territory) Grade 5

[Formerly course for building surveyors]

1. **Foreword**

The proposal concerns an interdisciplinary project [for students] in Grade 5.

The activity will be performed 3 h per week (possibly together), in the subjects: designing, topography, land evaluation, management and security of the building site. The project will be carried out by the curricular teachers and the workshops assistant, who will be the same for the four subjects. The project will be presented by the students during the state exam as PowerPoint and in the oral examination.

2. **Goals**

To acquire interdisciplinary competences through a project of requalification [renovation] of the area formerly Kennedy school, designated to become a canteen for students, tourists and workers.

3. **Objectives**

Knowledge	*Competences*
– To know the procedures, construction norms and the management of the building site in order to present a project – To know the PGT [government plan of the territory] norms at the end of the designing phase – To know the topographical methods of surveying – To know the theory of land valuation	– To execute a project of requalification – To execute a surveying layout. – To compose a metrical computation – To apply software PREGEO and DOCFA

(continued)

© The Editor(s) (if applicable) and The Author(s) 2019
D. Morselli, *The Change Laboratory for Teacher Training in Entrepreneurship Education*, SpringerBriefs in Education,
https://doi.org/10.1007/978-3-030-02571-7

(continued)

– To know the theory of real estate registry: making and conservation – To know the technical terms in English for report writing – To know the risks of building sites and the norms to refer to	– To estimate price of a building to be renovated – To write the building site PSC [security plan of the building site] – To execute the project report, both in Italian and English – To appraise a landscape (methodology)
Skills	*Habits*
– Work group – Project work – Problem-solving	– Initiative – Autonomy

4. **Time**

Three weekly hours, for a total amount of 99 h distributed in the following way: 24 h, land valuation and topography; 12 h, management of the building site; 40 h, designing. Plus 16 h during curricular time.

5. **Contents and timetable (h)**

Activity	Time (h)
Topography	
– Appraisal of the building to be renovated and of the neighbouring area	16
– Compiling the surveying update act through PREGEO software	8
Designing	
– Requalification project	30
– Metrical computation of requalification costs	10
Management of the building site	
– Risks of the building site	12
– Layout of the building site	
– PSC [security plan of the building site]	
Land valuation	
– Appraisal of existing vegetation	6
– Estimate of the pricing of the area through the transformation value	10
– Subscription into the real estate registry through DOCFA software	6
English	
– Writing the project report in English	8 h during curricular time
History	
– Historical and cultural analysis of the landscape where the building is situated	8 h during curricular time
Total amount	114

6. **Didactics methods**

- lectures
- elaboration of projects, reports, estimates
- files computations
- work in small groups: Internet search of documents and materials, discussions, reports and presentations writing
- didactic visits for surveying.

7. **Tests** (assessment contributes towards the marks of the involved disciplines in the report card)

- individual tests
- oral test
- interdisciplinary tests
- Evaluation of compositions, reports, estimates, presentations.

12 October 2016, The teachers

Appendix B
Results Validation

The diagram below summarizes the outcomes of the interviews and focus groups on the interdisciplinary project described in Chap. 5 in terms of features, potentials and challenges from four perspectives: teachers, workshop assistants, the Grade 5 class A and the Grade 5 class B. The bold is used for the sentences emerged from at least 3 different perspectives and the italics for the sentences emerged from 2 perspectives.

© The Editor(s) (if applicable) and The Author(s) 2019

D. Morselli, *The Change Laboratory for Teacher Training in Entrepreneurship Education*, SpringerBriefs in Education,
https://doi.org/10.1007/978-3-030-02571-7

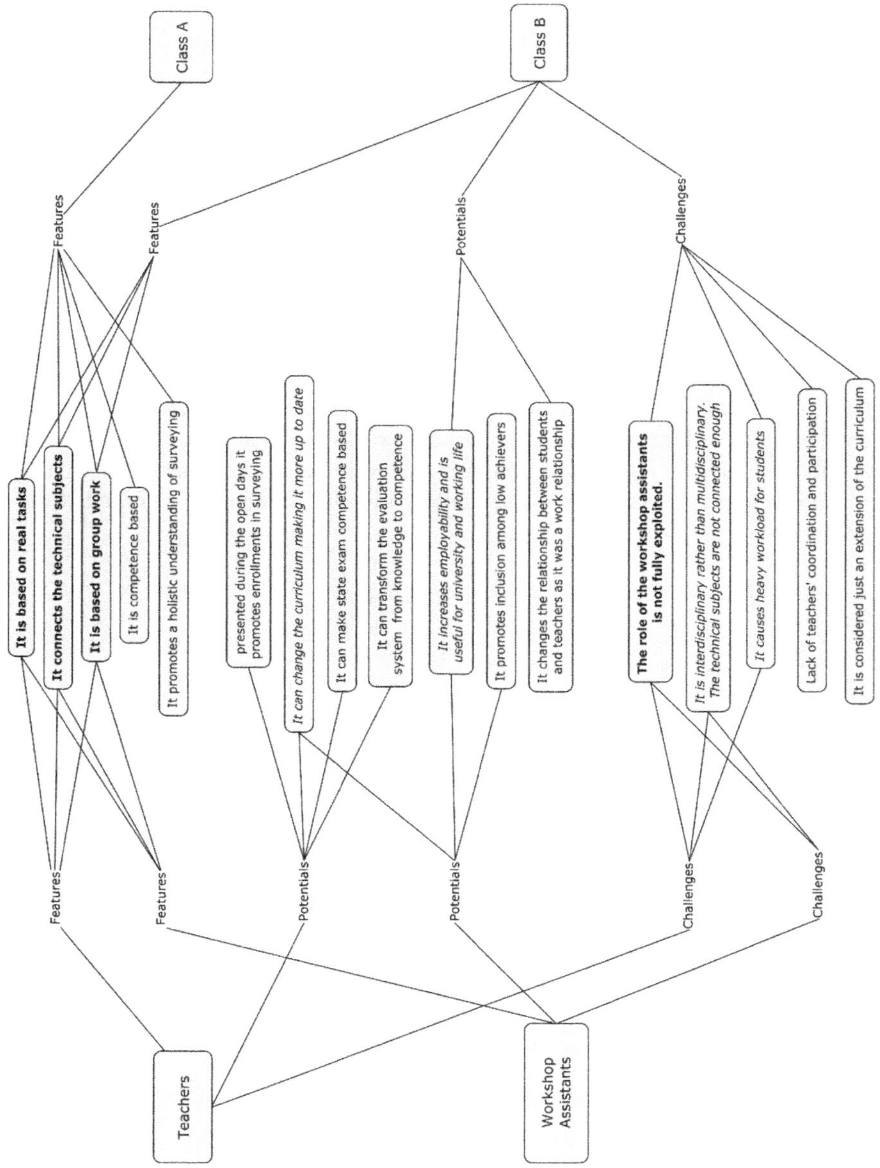

Class A
Class B
Features
Features
Potentials
Challenges
It is based on real tasks
It connects the technical subjects
It is based on group work
It is competence based
It promotes a holistic understanding of surveying
presented during the open days it promotes enrollments in surveying
It can change the curriculum making it more up to date
It can make state exam competence based
It can transform the evaluation system from knowledge to competence
It increases employability and is useful for university and working life
It promotes inclusion among low achievers
It changes the relationship between students and teachers as it was a work relationship
The role of the workshop assistants is not fully exploited.
It is interdisciplinary rather than multidisciplinary. The technical subjects are not connected enough
It causes heavy workload for students
Lack of teachers' coordination and participation
It is considered just an extension of the curriculum
Features
Features
Potentials
Potentials
Challenges
Challenges
Teachers
Workshop Assistants

Made in the USA
Las Vegas, NV
09 November 2024

11385108R00092